# Seeking Middle Ground
# on Social Security Reform

T0164423

*The Hoover Institution
gratefully acknowledges generous support from*

TAD AND DIANNE TAUBE
TAUBE FAMILY FOUNDATION
KORET FOUNDATION

*Founders of the Program on
American Institutions and Economic Performance*

*and Cornerstone gifts from*

SARAH SCAIFE FOUNDATION

# Seeking Middle Ground on Social Security Reform

*David Koitz*

HOOVER INSTITUTION PRESS
STANFORD, CALIFORNIA

www.hoover.org

Hoover Institution Press Publication No. 489

First printing, 2001

Manufactured in the United States of America

07 06 05 04 03 02 01    9 8 7 6 5 4 3 2 1

The paper used in this publication meets the minimum requirements of American National Standard for Information Sciences— Permanence of Paper for Printed Library Materials, ANSI Z39.48-1984. ⊚

Library of Congress Cataloging-in-Publication Data

Koitz, David.
Seeking middle ground on social security reform / David Koitz.
   p.   cm.
Includes bibliographical references and index.
ISBN 0-8179-9972-8 (alk. paper)
1. Social security—United States. I. Title.

HD7125.K5875 2001
368.4'3'00973—dc21                    2001016654

# Contents

# Acknowledgments

I wish to thank the Hoover Institution for funding the preparation of this monograph, and the Library of Congress for granting me a leave of absence. I am particularly grateful to John Raisian, the Hoover Institution's director, and John Cogan, one of its senior fellows, for inviting me to come out and work on this piece in their most wonderful environment, and for the gracious and ever-attentive support of the Hoover staff. I also appreciate the helpful comments and suggestions on the monograph's content from John Cogan and from Geoffrey Kollmann and Bill Robinson of the Congressional Research Service of the Library of Congress, and for the technical oversight of Pat Baker and Richard Sousa of the Hoover Institution.

The views and opinions expressed herein are solely mine and should not be considered views or recommendations of the Hoover Institution or the Library of Congress.

# CHAPTER 1

# Where We Are Today—
# The Setting for Reform

Perhaps at no time in the past half-century has the debate about social security been so introspective as it is now. Not since the inception of social security in 1935 and the consideration of a welfare-type alternative in 1950 has there been so much of a challenge to the role of government in providing the nation's workers with retirement benefits.[1] The principles of people earning federal "entitlements" by working, of requiring nearly universal worker participation, of compulsorily transferring income from workers to recipients through payroll taxation, and of paying benefits that favor low-wage earners and one-earner couples have remained deeply entrenched footings of the American social security system for nearly 65 years. Surely in a political sense, as measured by public acceptance and apparent opinion, the system has worked. There have been no social security tax revolts, and a whole industry of advocates has emerged to protect the benefits that past taxpayers believe they have earned with their "contributions."[2] When there has been serious talk of cutting federal taxes, it has rarely been about cutting social security's take—even with frequent concerns expressed about its size[3]—and any discourse about social security benefits is more typically about how to increase rather than reduce them.

This is not to suggest that there haven't been many criticisms levied against the system. Few, however, have captured policymakers' attention and tapped public discontent the way a variety of recent reform ideas have. The clash of policy concepts—social insurance versus wealth creation—is pronounced today. Social insurance in the United States was born in the 1930s, as a system that sought to insure society as a whole against poverty in old age—by some accounts, half or more of the aged were then living in some form of "dependency." Social insurance mandates participation while people work; it also dictates coverage of as many as the political system will permit, so that as few as possible will enter their later years dependent on welfare programs and their families. It requires contributions (taxes) but is less concerned about what the individual receives in return and more about the adequacy of the benefits it affords in general, the goal being to afford people with a minimal "floor of income protection" when they come to the point where they can no longer work.

Today's ardent proponents of reform see less need for a "governmental hand" and greater opportunities for workers to individually provide for their retirement years and potential disabilities, opportunities that offer greater choice and greater rewards both to individuals and the nation as a whole. This idea evolves in part from the philosophic belief that a system in which individuals are responsible for their own financial well-being would be fairer and, thus, economically beneficial to society as a whole. Proponents contend that the nation is much different today than in the past, with a much advanced financial infrastructure and capacity to sustain a viable individually based system that would be more enduring than a governmentally based income transfer program relying on taxes that may have to rise to unprecedented levels 30 years from now.

President Clinton heightened interest in reform with his last three State of the Union messages, calling particular attention to the system's long-range funding problems. He left the issue largely unattended, but his concerns served to complement a decade of warnings by the system's board of trustees—its presumed financial watchdogs—who routinely since 1989 have forecasted long-range funding shortfalls.[4] They also followed on the heels of warnings and promptings for action by two blue-ribbon commissions, a legislatively mandated advisory council, and a new social security advisory board, all of whom ruminated over the issues during the past six years.[5] Numerous members of Congress too, from both parties, have introduced a wide range of substantive reform bills since the 103rd Congress.

Despite this attention and calls for change, nothing of any notable significance has been done. The most recent Congress—the 106th—opened aggressively on the issue, with H.R.1 being set aside for President Clinton's anticipated proposal, but it closed on a hollow chord as no meaningful action was taken. The 2000 election campaign certainly kept the issue alive, but even with a change in executive leadership this year, it is not clear that the most relevant factors that thus far have bogged down the process will dissipate. Foremost among these issues is the presence of a tight governing balance in Washington. With the party composition of Congress remaining closely divided, the political setting has not changed. In addition, in contrast to the pressures leading up to past social security reforms, the system is not projected to have any near-term problems, even under adverse assumptions. Thus, no urgency exists.

What, then, will propel policymakers to come together? The last two major reforms of the Social Security system—enacted in 1977 and 1983—were driven by crises. In both instances, benefits would have had to be suspended or delayed within a few years or even months had Congress not acted. Admittedly, one important factor today is the passing of the 2000 election and the heightened partisanship it imposed on the legislative process. Policymakers now have a new "window of opportunity" in the first session of the 107th Congress and the first year of a new president's term of office.

However, even with this "fresh start," action will have to be swift if the midterm congressional elections of 2002 are not to get in the way. Moreover, it is quite possible that the partisanship of recent years has hardened ideological positions. Advocates of the current system, the liberal camp, like things the way they are. They recognize that there is some underlying discontent stemming from uncertainty about social security's long-range prospects, but by and large they view the system as the centerpiece of their ideological doctrine. From their perspective, they could accept the addition of a little revenue or the trimming of a few benefits (the latter only as a last resort), but not a real "fundamental" change. The "maintain benefits" theme reflected by their faction of the 1994–96 Social Security Advisory Council is the mantra.[6] Determined reform advocates, however, are looking to create a new system, something that is more individually based, less social, and with less governmental involvement. Patterning their proposals after recent changes occurring around the world, reformers see the current U.S. system as out of date and out of touch with modern society.

Led by President Clinton, who sidestepped recommending any structural change, Democrats in the 106th Congress generally (but not exclusively) adhered to the theme that the current system should be preserved. They took the position that with some "general fund" infusions, perhaps accompanied by investment of a portion of the social security trust funds in the stock market, the government would be able to pay the system's promised benefits—that is, its future commitments as prescribed by the "entitlement" rules of current law.[7] Republicans generally wanted to make substantive changes, but despite the introduction of many bills, fear of touching the "third rail of American politics" in a tight election year held them at bay. In the simplest terms, the two parties divided along lines of either (1) "the status quo is just fine" or (2) "it's time for something new."

Not all Democrats wanted to hold still, but these were in the minority. Certainly, Senators John Breaux, Bob Kerrey, Pat Moynihan, and Chuck Robb broke ranks from conventional party thinking with the introduction and co-sponsorship of major reform bills—bills that would have greatly reduced benefits for future recipients and substituted private savings accounts for some part of the system. Senator Breaux remains in the Senate; however, the other three have departed, and it is not clear which, if any, similar-minded Democrats will step up to take their places. From the other side of the aisle, not all Republicans wanted to replace the current system, but those wanting to move forward on the issue were held back, either by their own fear of political repercussions or the reticence of their leadership and caucus.

## THE LURE OF "FREE LUNCH"

President George W. Bush and the 107th Congress do have an opportunity to forge alliances, but with no prevailing sense of urgency, the desire to hold or retain control of the Congress with a small majority (by either party) may dampen the prospects for serious action. The campaigns leading up to the 2002 congressional elections leave only a year, perhaps 15 months, to find common ground. Republicans, in particular, are acutely aware of the damage they suffered in 1981 following a failed package of social security changes proposed by the Reagan administration, which by some accounts contributed to a significant loss of Republican House seats in the 1982 elections[8] and again in 1985 when Senate Republicans attempted to scale back cost of living adjustments (COLAs) in federal entitlement programs, including social security.[9] The hesitancy of their leadership team in the 106th Congress to give a "nod" to any substantive measures is testimony to the caution with which they approach social security.

How then could the ideological camps and political parties be brought together next year? If one camp wants no change and the other strives for an entirely new system, where is the middle ground? At least on the surface, Democrats and Republicans appear to be starting from more deeply divided positions than in 1981, when movement toward the last set of reforms began. Moreover, although appearing to want "something" more secure than the current system, the public does not seem to be exhibiting much conviction about where it wants the system to go. Opinion polls emanate both confusion and mixed messages. Liberal leaning pollsters generate evidence that the public likes the current system and does not want benefit cuts or tax increases. Conservative pollsters emphasize apprehension about the system's inability to meet its future commitments and support for individual retirement arrangements. The young seem to want a new system they can call their own, but older segments of the workforce want to preserve the benefits, or "rights" thereto, that they have earned thus far.

Hence, the opportune political quest of late has been for a "free lunch" scenario—*greater retirement security and an adequately financed social security system, all without prescribed benefit cuts or tax increases*. Although not promoted as such, "free lunch" was the reform image portrayed by both parties in the 106th Congress. President Clinton called only for using the government's general revenues from looming federal budget surpluses to shore up the system. Except for suggesting that recipients be allowed to work and collect full benefits and that aged survivors be given greater protections and/or larger benefits, he suggested neither future changes in the way benefits are calculated nor any constraints on eligibility. In the year leading up to his announcement of a reform plan, he emphasized and attempted to give credence to demographic projections pointing to an eventual shrinking of the number of workers supporting each recipient. Through a series of "town meeting" forums that President Clinton sponsored in 1998, he repeatedly brought attention to the potential fiscal strains of an aging population and the impending retirement of the post–World War II baby boom generation, of which he is one. However, when the year ended and it was time to put forth changes, he folded. Although not large in scope, the two benefit reforms he offered would actually cost money and, if anything, add to the financing inadequacy reflected in the trustees' projections.[10] There was not even a token benefit cut in his plan. Instead, he took the position that the government should pay down its privately held debt and credit the social security trust funds with savings from having done so.[11] In sum, his solution was to adopt general fund financing of the problem, and in such a way that he would effectively credit the trust funds twice for their impact on the debt.[12] The current law practice already would have credited the trust funds for surplus social security taxes received by the Treasury. The measure would in no way reduce the long-term costs of social security to the government, and although the "transfers" from the government's general fund might improve the public image of the social security ledgers—what its trust funds show—it would not generate additional income for the government. Nothing of value would actually be transferred because it would be a "paper" transaction between government accounts—it wouldn't provide the government with any direct means to meet the IOUs it gave to the trust funds during the earlier years of budget surpluses.

From an economic perspective, the part of the proposal calling for a reduction in the federal debt might appear preferable to consumption-directed tax cuts or new spending, but the plan would do little directly to address the structural turmoil surrounding the social security program. The Clinton administration repeatedly contended, however, that there would be long-term savings to the government from reduction or elimination of interest on the debt, savings that would make it easier for the government to eventually honor the IOUs given to the social security system.[13] In reality, the proposal represented nothing more than current law policy, that is, in the absence of any fiscal policy changes to lower taxes or increase spending, the surplus receipts would automatically go toward retiring the outstanding debt.

The Republicans offered little more. Their congressional leadership brushed off the Clinton proposal as not being meaningful reform, but offered up nothing substantive in its place. What they couldn't ignore, however, was the president's proposition to set the social security portion of the looming budget surpluses aside until the program's problems were addressed. President Clinton had broached this idea in his State of the Union address in 1998, and it rapidly gained momentum. It was a very successful form of posturing, and he incorporated it as the underlying fiscal policy theme in his FY1999, 2000, and 2001 budget submissions to Congress. The message was powerful because for decades the idea that the government was raiding the social security trust funds had been driven home to constituents by one politician after another. Simply stated, the public had been saturated with the notion that the trust funds had been misused. As a result, the president's theme rang true.

For a while, the idea of protecting the social security surpluses took on the aura of real reform and proved to be an effective device for the administration in thwarting the use of a large portion of the next 10 or 15 years' budget surpluses for other purposes, foremost among them being Republican-favored tax cuts. Pollsters serving both sides of the aisle said that "walling off" the social security surpluses had strong appeal with the voters. Not to be outdone, Republicans in Congress responded quickly, trying to portray themselves as the stauncher protectors of the system, with numerous legislative measures to "lock up" the system's share of the looming budget surpluses. They would keep policymakers, whoever they may be, from ever again raiding those funds.

With the focus redrawn, there were no substantive leadership-backed changes brought to the floor and no initiatives to raise social security taxes or cut its future outgo, not even for the creation of Republican-favored "personal" social security retirement accounts. For a brief period in 1999, there was a flurry of interest in a plan offered by Representatives Bill Archer and Clay Shaw, the chairmen of the House Ways and Means Committee and its Subcommittee on Social Security, respectively. Although they never introduced their plan in bill form, they had hoped to rouse support for it from both ideological camps by introducing an individual account component into social security as a means of financing "guaranteed" future social security benefits.[14] Initially anticipating the use of budget surpluses, the plan called for a governmental contribution equal to 2 percent of each worker's pay to be deposited annually by the Treasury Department into personal retirement accounts managed by private investment companies. The companies, in turn, would be required to invest the deposits in portfolios with a mandatory 60/40 investment split between equities and bonds. All covered workers would get an account with no additional contributions required of them, and the eventual annuities would be used (transferred to the social security trust funds) to finance some or all of the cost of each worker's future social security benefits. The sponsors argued that in some cases, albeit rare, workers could be better off than under current law—these being cases where the annuity payable from the account would exceed the worker's or survivor's social security benefit.[15] In effect, the plan would fix the system without raising taxes and without cutting benefits. As with the president's plan, it envisioned no pain.

Although recognized for its creative bent, the plan failed to garner the interest its sponsors had hoped for, with surprisingly loud opposition from conservative critics. The expectation was that linking an individual savings account to the current system would bring backing from conservative-minded reformers and that "guaranteeing" future "current law" social security benefits would leave the system's liberal protectors without a basis to protest. Not only would the system's financing problem be resolved, but also its benefit structure would be preserved.[16] Instead, conservative reformers reacted negatively, contending that the plan did not really create personal accounts, that it would not give "real" assets to future retirees, and that it merely represented a backdoor way of preserving the existing system and creating a new federal entitlement that would serve only to raise the government's future costs and role in the provision of retirement income.[17] With the conservatives taking a harsh tone, liberal critics did not feel compelled to raise a strong dissent. A few, however, were concerned that the plan might be appealing to some of their own congressional supporters, particularly as social security benefits would be "unaffected."[18] The administration remained relatively muted.[19] Although hearings were held, no action was taken to move the plan.

## CAN THE VARIOUS "IDEALS" BE JOINED?

It is probably fair to say that part of the issue's overall complexity is in deciphering what ideals each side is striving for. If they could dictate their own prescription, what would each want? What do liberals and conservatives really want? Is it mostly a debate about the role of government, with liberals seeking to keep what they have and conservatives seeking to reduce what they perceive as too much government intrusion in people's lives?

To some extent it is, at least in terms of fiscal policy. President's Clinton's strategy of using budget surpluses, notably the social security portion of them, to buy down the outstanding federal debt is as much ideological as economic. Buying down the debt does nothing in and of itself to shore up the social security system.

Whether the government uses excess social security receipts to increase other spending, lower other taxes, or buy down the debt
doesn't alter the fact that as a fiscal policy choice, it is not using
them for social security purposes. What the strategy does is preserve the overall federal tax base, and to that extent, it preserves
resources for government programs. Debt reduction could easily
fall out of favor. Moreover, President Clinton's plan did not
change anything about the nature of social security. Thus, the governmental role of the system in the provision of retirement income
would be similarly preserved.

Republicans, on the other hand, typically want less government,
especially on matters where they believe society has the capacity
and people have or are given the opportunity to take care of themselves.[20] From the Republican perspective, setting money aside for
retirement, death, and disability does not have to be done through
a massive governmental program. The belief is that private systems
and institutions do exist today in a much more sophisticated and
extensive way than in 1935 to allow people to save on their own,
and people can be required by law to do so in the same way they
are told to pay taxes to the government. If employers, including
the federal government, can effectively operate 401(k) or similar
plans for their employees, there is no real reason why the vast
middle class of Americans can't provide for their "core" retirement benefits through ownership and accumulation of their own
assets. Republicans feel that the overall level of taxation is too
high, especially during this era of budget surpluses, and to continue to generate excess taxes under the theme that they are needed
for debt reduction is simply a pretense as well as an invitation for
maintaining if not increasing the level of government spending.

THE LIBERAL DEFENDERS' CASE

For liberal defenders of social security, the infusion of general revenues into the system is a facade for reform. Building a larger trust
fund with general fund infusions would not involve a real transfer
of money, nor would it store assets away; it would simply create
future IOUs that the government would have to honor. It would

make social security's ledgers look healthier, but it would leave the obvious question of where the government would get the money to make good on the IOUs. Whether the government would give IOUs to the system today or wait to raise taxes or reduce spending tomorrow, a critical question is left unanswered—where exactly would the resources come from to cover the long-range shortfall?

Many who advocate general fund infusions really don't want the system to change. They fear that the substantive options for restoring the system's solvency—cutting benefits and raising taxes—will only intensify public distrust and skepticism about its longevity. The aversion to general revenues dates back to the program's inception. President Franklin Roosevelt stated, *"I believe the funds necessary to provide this insurance should be raised by contribution rather than by an increase in general taxation."*[21] *"With those payroll taxes, no damned politician can ever scrap my social security program."*[22] Even some who advocate general fund infusions fear their use if they were to be of a significant magnitude. Drawing resources away from other governmental programs could eventually lead to means testing of social security benefits as policymakers question why scarce governmental resources are being used to supplement the leisure lifestyles of too many well-to-do retirees. They also fear that means testing could be the final undoing of the program. Means testing is demeaning; it smacks of welfare and discourages private savings. Eventually, they fear, public sentiment would turn negative and lead to the program's demise.

Liberal defenders also stress that there is no immediate crisis and contend that the point of the system's insolvency is so far off—projected to be 36 years from now—that it is meaningless. They argue that *"since the system's not broken, it doesn't need fixing."* They feel strongly that social security is an antipoverty program first and foremost, that it always has been, and that it should continue to be. At a rudimentary level, they take the view that *"too many people left to their own devices will 'screw up' before reaching retirement,"* and society will be back where it started in the 1930s, with widespread aged poverty. They like the re-distributive nature of the system; they like the fact that the government is involved (they perceive it to be more of a guarantee—a benevolent government bestowing "earned" benefits); and they like the politics of social security (i.e., social activism can pressure elected representatives into doing things that private enterprise wouldn't). Ideally, they would savor trustees' reports that show no financing problems exist near or far, and if they could get people to accept an alternative view of the future (than the trustees'), they would change the long-range economic or demographic assumptions to avoid having to say there is a problem.[23] Some take solace in the fact that while the magnitude of the long-range deficit is significant enough to raise concerns, the projected problem has stopped growing, and in fact has diminished slightly in the last three trustees' reports.[24]

Their suggestion to invest the trust funds in the financial markets is not so much an idea to "rescue" the system as it is a counter-proposal to those wanting to divert the flow of social security taxes into individual accounts. They argue, *"If the stock market is such a good thing for people individually, why don't we invest the social security trust funds in them?"* If taken at face value, their supposition is that we can leverage the system's surpluses—substituting higher yielding stocks for federal bonds—and thereby increase its investment return. In some respects, this could be viewed as a sop to those wanting to substantively address the financing problems, the argument being, *"We don't need to raise taxes or cut benefits; all we need to do is change how we invest the trust funds."*

From a more searching perspective, the idea rests on the supposition that society can grow its way around the fiscal strains of becoming "older." It certainly is more of a response than crediting the trust funds with general fund infusions; the government would be holding and accumulating real assets. But if the social security actuaries expressed an unwillingness, or what few would question as a valid uncertainty, about how such a change would alter the system's investment return, the system's advocates would likely see little merit in the idea and oppose it.[25] Pragmatically, however, the idea suffers from a fundamental disconnection with the principles of a free enterprise society—it begs the question of how exactly the government could become a shareholder in the nation's businesses without eventually dictating how and what those businesses do.

Ideally, what many liberal protectors of the system want is the status quo. They hope for or desire a change in events and assumptions, perhaps a continuing robust economy feeding on technological advances that propel productivity, from higher immigration or birth rates, even from a change in actuarial methods, any or all of which could eventually turn adverse trustees' forecasts into positive ones.[26] From this perspective, obfuscation may not restore public confidence—and that would be a negative—but for some it is preferable to engaging in a political exercise to make changes to the system that they may not be able to control.

## THE CONSERVATIVE REFORMERS' PERSPECTIVE

The most ardent of conservative reformers want a new system entirely, one that responds more directly to the actions that individuals take for themselves. They see no good reason why workers can't save on their own and view the current system, with its large array of social features, as a holdover from the depression era. "Social insurance" may have had a purpose then, but not to the same extent today in a fully employed, technologically based society. Conservative reformers want a new system for a new time, one that allows for wealth creation—never before a premise of social security. In contrast to the belief of the system's defenders, they contend that people can plan and set aside money for their own retirement. They believe that the current system is built too clumsily on a sense of ownership and that under a new system of individually based accounts people will get what they have really earned. Poverty concerns, they argue, should be addressed through welfare programs, not by a national retirement system based on workers' contributions. Use of general revenues to support welfare is fine, but not the use of personal contributions in the form that people now perceive their social security taxes to be. Conservative reformers feel that people have been living with a myth that they will get what they paid for from the current system—a myth perpetuated by politicians whose tenure is best assured by preserving the view that the system is equitable. Ideally, conservative reformers want a rapid conversion to a very different form of preparing for retirement and disability.

What many fail to fully appreciate is how imbedded the current system is in American society. The idea that social security is there for the parents of today's workers is deeply entrenched. A worker may complain about his or her social security tax levy, but if then asked if social security benefits should be cut, the conventional polling response is "no." The fact that one in six people in the population receives social security benefits, that census bureau surveys suggest it represents up to 40 percent of the income of the elderly, and that 50 percent or more of the elderly rely on it for more than half of their income are powerful arguments confronting a politician candidly weighing opportunities for reform. How does one contest those wanting to preserve the system when it is so easy for them to justify or rationalize its worthiness?

Perhaps one could use the "moneys' worth" argument. Certainly younger workers feel they can do better by investing their social security taxes on their own. Coupling increased public awareness of the declining returns that a "mature" pay as you go system is capable of achieving with the general skepticism the public holds about the system's future, the notion that younger segments of society are paying their "contributions" into an unworthy system has become fairly pervasive. Even this is a cause of concern for defenders of the system, some of whom fear it is an Achilles' heel.

Regardless of the merits of their case, however, critics of the system too often fail to recognize the issues of transitioning. Society is not debating the merits of embarking on some new role for government—that is, the first-time provision of a national retirement system. It decided to do so in 1935 and put the idea in motion in 1937, when social security taxes were first levied. The system is now a monolith, the single largest spending activity of the federal government. It is a huge money machine recycling $500 billion through the economy from workers to recipients. One can envision an alternative, perhaps many alternatives—as many of the system's critics have—but a democratic society cannot dismantle an institution of this magnitude overnight. A $500 billion retirement program, in existence for more than 60 years, around which millions of workers have built long-term claims, cannot be cast aside in pursuit of an entirely new system, certainly not without a torrent of discontent.

## THE PERPLEXING "TRANSITION" ISSUE

Putting philosophic issues aside, the point is that it is hardly a technical matter to overcome the transition issues of adopting a new system. If workers are allowed or required to divert their social security taxes into individual accounts, where will the money come from to continue to meet the obligations of the current system? Social security receipts are currently in excess of the system's expenditures, but not by such large amounts, nor for such a lengthy period (until 2015 under the latest projections), that the system could absorb a large and long-term diversion of taxes. Moreover, immediately diverting taxes would only accelerate the point of the system's projected insolvency. In effect, if large amounts of social security taxes are diverted, it threatens the system. Workers who do divert their taxes could be asked to forfeit their eventual social security claims, but there are still 45 million people collecting benefits now, and older workers nearing retirement are not likely to want to give up their prospective claims. Those older workers have already contributed large amounts to the system, they are close to their potential retirement years, and they don't have time to build a large alternative nest egg on their own. Those most likely to opt for a new system (assuming participation was optional) would be the young, and even though there might be savings to the old system in the long run if they were required to forfeit some or all of their eventual benefits, the savings would not occur for many years, perhaps long after the point of insolvency was reached, and thereby would be meaningless as an offset to the lost revenues.

Diverting large amounts to individual accounts would also impair any effort to reduce the government's outstanding debt. This may not appear as serious a political impediment to the proposal as a threat to the payment of benefits, but it is not an inconsequential issue in the current climate when so many promises have been made about using surplus budget receipts to reduce or retire the debt.

Some have suggested that the transitioning issue could be overcome by not waiting to curtail benefit promises, by phasing in benefit reductions now sufficient to offset the revenue diversion. Under this approach, individual accounts might be automatically set up for *all* workers, even older workers, thereby creating a mechanism under which they could build up alternative assets for retirement. However, this approach may only serve to raise concerns about inadequate benefit levels for those now approaching retirement—the oldest baby boomers. Social security benefit reductions that would be phased in to offset the revenue diversion may have to be on top of reductions already needed to help bring the system's long-term income and outgo into balance. It takes years of contributions and compounding of asset earnings to build a significant accumulation. Baby boomers will begin collecting social security in 2008, in only seven years, certainly not a lengthy time to build a sizeable nest egg.

In sum, although workers' concerns about the falling value of paying into social security may be a catalyst for reform, critics of the system need to focus on the practicality of their ideas. How to effectively transition—both in terms of keeping the current system financed and affording retirees in the transition period with adequate benefit levels—is at the heart of the debate. Moreover, although younger workers may grow increasingly receptive to reform, the portion of the population having a direct stake in the current system is also growing. The closer the baby boomers get to retirement, the greater the proportion is of the population with a vested interest in the status quo.

## SOME THREADS OF COMMON GROUND

Although little direction can be found in the prescriptions offered by President Clinton and the actions taken by the 106th Congress, some fragments of common ground can be gleaned from the political forays that transpired. Among them is the emergence of unified federal budget surpluses and the broad support for using them in some fashion to alter social security. In the preceding era of budget deficits, the only resources policymakers could imagine using were those attributable to social security—that's where the surpluses were, at least on paper. For Democrats, there had been no surplus governmental receipts to infuse into the system—no "real" revenue excesses—and the social security surpluses that arose were already being credited to the system. For Republicans, to suggest using the social security surpluses for individual accounts meant worsening the budget deficits and robbing the social security system of "future" resources it could ill afford to lose.

With the subsequent emergence of budget surpluses, "real" surplus receipts, the dialogue has changed immensely. Although Republicans prefer to think of budget surpluses as unnecessary taxation and call for tax cuts and Democrats prefer to preserve the tax base and have latched onto the theme of using the excess receipts for debt reduction, both camps have accepted an earmarking or reserving of what is viewed as the social security system's portion of them. Of some $4.6 trillion in cumulative budget surpluses projected for the 2001–2010 period, some $2.4 trillion have been rhetorically earmarked for debt reduction, with both parties promising not to touch the latter until social security reform is enacted.[27]

A pronouncement by both parties of their willingness to do this is not in and of itself a plan for change, but it does reflect the priority each gives to holding trillions of dollars in budget decisions at bay, which they have done for three years. It was an extremely effective political message in the 106th Congress for both parties because for decades the notion that social security could not truly be separated from the rest of the federal budget was generally viewed as an inescapable consequence of the fiscal condition of the government—excess social security dollars flowed into the U.S. Treasury, offsetting the deficit occurring with the rest of the government's activities.[28] As projections of budget surpluses emerged and grew larger over the past three years, contentiousness erupted over the use of non–social security surpluses—over the use of the so-called "on budget" portion—but at least the part attributable to social security has given policymakers a common cache of initial resources around which to begin a dialogue.[29] That said, the true test of their significance might come if a sizeable recession emerges in the near future, eroding the magnitude of the excess receipts.

Another potentially adhesive factor is the turnover of political leaders. It offers a change in format, a new venue. It's the change not just in control of the White House but also in congressional leadership and the respective authorizing committees. Three of the four chairmen and ranking minority members of the House Ways and Means and Senate Finance Committees—the committees of each body of Congress with principal jurisdiction over social security matters—Representative Bill Archer and Senators Pat Moynihan and Bill Roth, have left. In addition, it is not uncommon for subcommittee chairmen to change chairs as new Congresses begin. New committee leaders often want to be assertive, as a show of strength, to solidify their positions, to avoid being put on a defensive track, and to reflect the sense of responsibility they feel—they quickly find that they are the perceived congressional authorities on the issues at hand. Wanting to make his own forceful mark, Representative Jake Pickle used social security's looming financial problems to his advantage in 1980 upon becoming the Democratic chairman of the Ways and Means' Social Security Subcommittee. The constant pressure he exerted on his own party and the Reagan administration kept the then projected insolvency of the system high on the congressional agenda and eventually helped to force the Reagan administration and Pickle's colleagues to face up to the issue. As chairman of a subcommittee with "authority to legislate," he rapidly forged alliances with Republicans on the subcommittee and pushed for a bipartisan approach to shore up the system early in 1981—even in the absence of backing from his Democratic leadership. Once established as the "reform-minded" chairman, for the next two years he kept pushing until action was finally taken in the spring of 1983. Although less successful, both Representatives Jim Bunning and Clay Shaw exhibited a similar desire to tackle the issue when they assumed their respective Republican chairmanships of the same subcommittee in 1995 and 2000. They both showed a strong desire to make their mark on the program early in their tenure.

Perhaps equally important and complementing the potential thrusts from new committee leadership is the fact that there has been bipartisan interest in reform shown by a considerable number of members of both the Ways and Means and Finance Committees. Both sides of the committees understood the respective positions their parties had taken in the 106th Congress, but both clearly acknowledged the system's problems and expressed a desire to move on them. In opening remarks to Chairman Archer at a 1999 hearing on the Archer-Shaw plan and other bills, the ranking Democrat on the committee, Charlie Rangel, made the point this way:

> As we listen to all of these plans, I do hope, at some point either at our hearings or at meetings that you would be inclined to call, that we can develop a process that could lead us toward bipartisanship, because I know that you agree that the only way that we can tackle this is in a bipartisan manner. It is not going to be done on C-SPAN, and it is not going to get done with these mikes in front of us. We have to find out what areas of agreement and disagreement we have. We have an opportunity to pick apart the President's plan . . . and will also be able to find some flaws in the Archer-Shaw plan, but while we are doing this, I do hope that the membership will keep a positive view in mind, because after we have found the flaws, we have the responsibility to pick up the pieces and move forward.[30]

On the Senate side, two of the eleven Republican (Senators Grassley and Thompson) and four of the nine Democratic members (Senators Breaux, Kerrey, Moynihan, and Robb) of the Finance Committee sponsored or co-sponsored substantive social security reform bills that included measures to not only create individual accounts but also scale back the current program's long-range expenditures and raise receipts. In addition, although not presenting his idea in the form of a bill, a third committee Republican, Senator Phil Gramm, publicized a major reform approach he wanted to pursue. The Republican chairman too, Senator Bill Roth, introduced a bill to use budget surpluses to create government-funded individual accounts for all social security taxpayers, recognizing that eventually social security benefits may have to be constrained to make the system solvent.

Still another factor lending momentum to the issue is the heightened attention the presidential candidates gave it. New presidents upon entering office typically move quickly on their major campaign themes, and both candidates called for changes to social security. Both wanted to present themselves and their parties as activists on the issue. Vice President Gore, like President Clinton, suggested using general revenues to shore up the system, supplemented by new voluntary accounts for moderate and low-income workers. Governor Bush suggested allowing all workers to bolster their retirement income through new personal accounts funded with a portion of their social security taxes, along with other measures, formulated by a bipartisan panel, to shore up the current system. Most interesting is that although they wanted to contrast themselves from each other, their reform messages were not dramatically different. Both accepted the fact that there is a potential long-term problem to solve. Neither suggested disturbing the promises of current recipients or those nearing retirement. Neither espoused creating an entirely new system. Both saw the creation of individual accounts as part of an eventual package to shore up future retirement incomes. Both acknowledged that budget surpluses offer a unique financing opportunity. And both wanted to restore public confidence. Granted, there was a lot of detail left unsaid, but neither showed a desire to distinguish himself either as a radical reformer or as one who is totally comfortable with the status quo.

Finally, there is an underlying unease among many policymakers, and perhaps the public, about losing time. From governmental entities to private business and advocacy groups, the call for action has been fairly uniform. Few who are close to the issue contest the existence of a problem (even if only projected). With the first wave of baby boomer retirements less than a decade away, there is growing sentiment, maybe apprehension, that delaying action will only make it more difficult to accomplish as the ranks of those with an immediate stake in the system swell. In dozens of congressional hearings since 1995, a chorus of witnesses has echoed the conclusion of the various social security trustees that the sooner action is taken the better. Although the legislative response has been sparse thus far, close to a hundred bills were introduced in the 106th Congress seeking either to "save" or "reform" the system or to "protect" its surpluses pending consideration of reform.

## IF THERE IS IDEOLOGICAL COMMON GROUND, IT IS NOT APPARENT

Common ground on the issue is certainly not in the center of the debate. However, there may be some on the fringes. The recognition that the current system potentially suffers from a long-range financing imbalance is bipartisan. Since passage of the last social security rescue plan in 1983, eight Republican- and eight Democratic-led boards of trustees have projected long-term financing shortfalls. Both parties have heightened the issue in recent years. Both maintain that there is a need for a national retirement system, and both see the advantages of increasing national savings as a means of continuing one.

Democrats would have to stretch to accept a system of individual accounts, although President Clinton and Vice President Gore opened the door to the idea of a limited role. At a minimum for both parties, there is considerable appeal to making such accounts available to those who don't have such options today through their employment (through 401(k)s or related defined contribution arrangements). Both parties would have to stretch to make explicit changes to the current social security system—benefit constraints or tax increases—but a number of members of Congress from both parties have introduced bills to do so. Congressional Republicans fear taking the lead, but at the same time they would have to stretch not to accept them if supported by Democrats, regardless of whatever political advantage they might afford. Using general revenues also would be a stretch for Republicans, particularly if advanced as the single or principal measure of reform (as President Clinton did and Vice President Gore advocated), but various Republican members have proposed doing so as a "transition" mechanism or to fill a gap in their more far-reaching plans. Republicans would similarly have to stretch to accept investing the trust funds in the stock market. For them (as well as some Democrats), it would require breaking a fundamental precept about the role of government and the private sector. However, the momentum for such and the impediment it poses toward reform may have waned. Although advocated by President Clinton and vocal elements on the liberal side, the public has not embraced such a policy—the fear of government intrusion in private enterprise is strong.

Ultimately, for meaningful action to occur, both parties and ideological camps would have to compromise on their respective positions about the role of government and the role of the individual. For the public, much of that debate is an "inside the beltway" exercise. For most people, the issue is less about the survival of social security and more about the achievement of economic security and greater assurance of having adequate resources in retirement. Understanding that there are risks in all forms of planning and preparing for retirement—that no system, public or private, can truly provide guarantees—is a first step. Too much of the recent dialogue has preyed upon the public's innate fears—fear of the financial market's collapse or fear of unachievable government promises. For something meaningful to the public to be achieved, the dialogue will have to change. It will have to focus less on the central ideals of each party and more on drawing out the advantages and minimizing the risks of the basic policy choices each advances.

# CHAPTER 2

# The Resilient Long-Range Problem

The image of a social security program with financial problems probably dates back to the early 1970s. Through the first half of its 65-year existence, the social security program operated with a fairly healthy outlook, at least as portrayed by its trustees. A majority of the nation's workers were covered almost immediately, but only a small segment of the population was initially eligible for benefits. Hence, in its infancy, the program was flush with revenues and its outgo was minimal. As time passed, the number of eligible recipients grew as more and more workers who had paid social security taxes reached retirement age or left eligible survivors, but the system's income and trust fund balances ballooned with the burgeoning economy of World War II and the postwar economic restructuring and reforms. Legislation enacted in 1950 also was pivotal; from that point on, the program grew not only from the natural maturing of a still young retirement system but also from periodic legislative amendments expanding its benefit categories and the level of payments—all of which were financed with forecasts of future surpluses or increases in taxes policymakers thought sufficient to cover the new spending. It was a different era than today—raising taxes, expanding coverage, and adding new benefits were not insurmountable obstacles for policymakers pursuing a course of incremental expansionism.

## THE 1970s—THE ERA OF EXPANSIONISM RECEDES
## AS FINANCING PROBLEMS EMERGE

The 1970s changed all that. The program's benefit rolls reached a nearly mature state as a number of generations of covered workers entered their retirement years and were receiving benefits,[31] its trust fund balances had dwindled as a percent of annual expenditures and it became more of a "pay as you go" system, and the long-range economic and demographic trends that had always given the system a sort of submerged financing cushion evaporated.[32] Following a major set of amendments in 1972/73—including the enactment of automatic annual benefit increases—the long era of expansion ended abruptly. The 1974 trustees' report incorporated new data from the 1970 census showing that the post–World War II baby boom had ended; this converged with a significant tempering of long-range assumptions about economic growth.[33] In the eight-year period prior to the 1974 report, five benefit increases had been enacted, cumulatively raising benefits by 83 percent.[34] This was followed by a recession, a crushing period of inflation, and stagnant wages. The report reflected a long-range average deficit of 2.98 percent of the nation's aggregate covered and taxable payrolls—an amount equal to about 27 percent of the sys-

DECLINE IN SOCIAL SECURITY RESERVES, 1945–1980

| Year | Trust fund balances— number of years' worth of expenditures on hand |
|------|--------------------------------------------------------------------|
| 1945 | 17.0 |
| 1950 | 7.0 |
| 1955 | 3.7 |
| 1960 | 1.8 |
| 1965 | 1.0 |
| 1970 | 1.0 |
| 1975 | 0.6 |
| 1980 | 0.2 |

Social Security Administration; balances at end of year compared to following year's outgo

tem's projected average income. Just two years earlier, the trustees had projected a small long-range surplus.

Further aggravating the situation was a flaw built into the automatic benefit increase provision—authorizing automatic annual cost of living adjustments, or COLAs—enacted the previous year. Although intended to keep the value of benefits from being eroded by inflation as recipients got older, it had the unintended effect of also raising the eventual initial benefits of people not yet retired. Their benefits would have been expected to rise in any event because each new cohort would have had higher wage records than the last; however, with the coupling of their higher wage records with the automatic adjustments made to the "benefit table" in the law (from which their benefit levels would be derived), a dramatic increase in the level of new benefit awards emerged. In the 20-year period leading up to 1970, workers retiring at age 65 with a career of "average" earnings could expect to receive initial benefits that represented between 30 and 35 percent of their final earnings. By 1975, the figure had risen to 42 percent (more than 25 percent higher than that of the comparable 1960 retiree), and by 1980, to 51 percent (some 55 percent higher than the 1960 retiree).[35] Had Congress not stepped in and changed the benefit computation rules in 1977, the figure might have grown to 67 percent for a comparable retiree in the year 2000. Moreover, as a consequence of the large inflation-driven COLAs and escalating initial benefits, the system was facing the possibility that one of its trust funds would be totally depleted by 1978 (the other, in 1983), leaving it unable to meet its immediate benefit commitments. Its projected long-range costs were likewise ballooning. The 1977 trustees' report forecasted that they would grow from a little under 11 percent of taxable payroll then to 27.5 percent in 2051. The average long-range deficit for the 1977–2051 period was projected to be 8.2 percent of payroll, a deficiency equal to 75 percent of the system's average income.

## THE 1980s—RESCUE AGAIN AND THEN EROSION

Even with resolution of the technical problem with the benefit rules, and the enactment of other measures to shore up social security's financing (including both short- and long-run increases in taxes), Congress still left the system with a sizeable long-range deficit, one that was only a little lower than the size of the deficit currently projected.[36] They could not find enough measures around which to form a consensus to eliminate the entire shortfall. Moreover, in the near-term, they left only a small margin of annual surpluses and trust fund balances to tide the program over. When a new bout of inflation subsequently emerged, followed by back-to-back recessions in 1981 and 1982, the system again confronted potential near-term insolvency, and the long-range problem left over by the 1977 changes was still hanging (albeit, now somewhat larger).

Hence, in 1981, Congress again began an arduous search for remedies, a search that was complicated by having a split in control of its two chambers—Republicans had taken over the Senate, while the House remained in Democratic hands, although weakened in numbers. Early in 1981, there was substantial interest in addressing the social security issue in the House Ways and Means Committee, but it was complicated and short-circuited by an overly aggressive set of benefit reductions proposed by the Reagan administration in May of that year. The May package had come on the heels of a number of controversial social security benefit constraints that the administration had proposed in its February budget plan—its first budget upon taking over the White House—including eliminating a long-standing minimum benefit for some three million *current* recipients.

The May package backfired badly. It ran into a buzz saw of discontent, especially because of a provision to reduce "early retirement" benefits (those payable at age 62) by 44 percent beginning as soon as the following January. The public reacted quickly and harshly. Even Republican leaders in the Senate were forced to pass a resolution questioning the package.[37]

The summer months brought charges back and forth that Republicans were trying to dismantle social security. The budget and May reform proposals gave ample ammunition to the program's defenders, who took advantage of the public's strong disapproval. The partisan charges brought the Ways and Means Committee reform efforts to a halt as the issue gave Democrats a new offense. The Reagan administration had come into office and immediately swept a major tax cut package through the Congress. It was the pinnacle piece of their economic program. It was only in their efforts to offset some of the revenue losses that resistance emerged, particularly over social security changes, and even then, the bulk of their proposals were eventually enacted with some modifications. Playing the social security card, however, gave Democrats a way of eroding the momentum of the administration's early successes.[38]

With the Ways and Means Committee's efforts held in check, the ball was clearly in the administration's court. It had broached the social security issue unsuccessfully, and the burden of quelling the discontent was left in its hands. In a nationally televised address in September 1981, President Reagan withdrew the May package, proposed the formation of a bipartisan blue-ribbon commission to address the issue, and called for enactment of an "interfund borrowing" authority to tide the program over while the commission did its work.[39] By December 1981, a deal with congressional leaders of both parties had been reached, and an executive order formed the 15-member National Commission on Social Security Reform, headed by Alan Greenspan.

The commission held numerous hearings and meetings in 1982, methodically addressing many of the issues, but as with Congress, it was plagued by acrimonious debate and partisanship through most of the period leading up to the 1982 elections. The House Democratic Study Group, a liberal-leaning faction of the party, had gone so far as to paint an entire history of Republican antipathy toward the program.[40] Even when the election passed, the commission had difficulty moving itself forward. Under its charter, it only had until December 31, 1982, to complete its work, and reportedly, it was only with the efforts of a small bipartisan group of its members and administration representatives that an eventual agreement was struck in early January 1983. Even then, the commision was not able to get a full consensus for its recommendations, particularly those directed at the long-term problem.[41] Another inter-fund borrowing authority also was enacted late in 1982, designed to keep the program from becoming insolvent before July 1983, while Congress and the administration considered the commissions' recommendations.

Sticking close to the framework of the commission's deal, the Congress and administration were able to forge an agreement on both short- and long-range measures fairly quickly, measures involving both revenue increases and benefit constraints—including eventually raising the age for full social security benefits from 65 to 67 (phasing in beginning in the year 2000) and, for the first time, partial income taxation of benefits. In less than four months, the authorizing committees, the two chambers, and President Reagan signed off on the Social Security Amendments of 1983, a package of changes projected to resolve the system's entire financing problem. A decade of adverse trustees' reports had finally been brought to a close.

As it turned out, however, the aura of success was relatively short-lived. The program did grow sizeable surpluses in the 1980s from a much more robust economy than had been projected in 1983,[42] but within two years after enactment, new long-range problems surfaced, and within six years, they were large enough to draw warnings again from trustees serving in the Bush administration.

In some respects, the re-emergence of long-range deficits was inevitable. When deliberating on the 1983 amendments, Congress gave little attention to how the new provisions would affect the system's financial flows year by year or decade by decade after 1990. The focus was almost exclusively on assuring the system could meet its commitments over the next 10 years and *on average* over the next 75. The fact that the average 75-year imbalance was remedied by having large surpluses in the early decades followed by large deficits later went largely unnoticed. Congress did not consider the fact that as each year passed, a surplus year would be dropped from the front end of the projections and a deficit year would be added at the back. In effect, the 1983 amendments had left a built-in mechanism for eventually portraying future deficits again.[43]

In addition, other circumstances and assumptions changed. The system's disability rolls expanded, and long-range assumptions were adjusted accordingly. The "real wage" gains of workers had continued to slip, leading to a drop in the long-range 1.5 percent annual growth rate assumed in 1983 to the 1 percent rate currently assumed. The proportion of assumed future compensation subject to taxation also was reduced to reflect a gradual rise in other non-taxable forms of compensation (among them, employer-sponsored health insurance). Finally, actuarial methods were greatly revised and had a noticeably large negative impact. Surprisingly, revised demographic assumptions actually worked to the system's advantage, as higher immigration, slower improvement in female mortality, and higher near-term fertility rates offset a reduction in long-term fertility assumptions. Nonetheless, when taken as a whole, the revised assumptions added to a gradually rising long-range deficit and a projection of trust fund insolvency at some point in the latter portion of the baby boomers' retirement years.

When looked at in retrospect from a policymaking perspective, the years from 1983 to 2000 were relatively calm. There was only modest, piecemeal legislative action, and although the long-range projections gradually deteriorated, the short-range situation improved significantly, benefiting from two sustained spells of economic growth. Inflation was held in check throughout the period, and only one recession, in 1990, arose to impair the system's revenue stream. The 17-year period was so tranquil that three quadrennial advisory councils, one in 1984, another in 1988, and a third in 1991, did not even focus on the social security system's financing situation, directing themselves instead to national health care concerns, medicare, and disability issues.

## THE 1990s—"ENTITLEMENTS" EMERGE AS THE ISSUE

The most controversial events affecting the program revolved around its treatment under the federal budget. Huge budget deficits arising in the 1980s kept constant pressure on fiscal policymakers to seek budget constraints, and a number of attempts were made in the mid-1980s to include social security cutbacks in deficit-reduction or budget balancing bills. Most prominent were proposals to constrain the size of social security and other entitlement

COLAs. None affecting social security, however, were ultimately enacted. Although concerns mounted about the long-range growth in federal entitlements, the principal focus of congressional policy-makers was on how reining in such programs could potentially contribute to a balanced budget in the near term. Even with this attention, however, Congress eventually backed away from social security cuts and even went to considerable lengths to shield the program from budget-motivated reductions, including repeatedly enacting provisions to take the program "off budget." Throughout the 1990s, social security remained a prominent fixture in shaping fiscal policy, but mostly because its surpluses were viewed as a means of offsetting deficits in the rest of the budget.

There was, however, an undercurrent of concern building. With each passing year, beginning in 1989, the trustees reported average long-range deficits in excess of their usual tolerance of 5 percent of income; the deficit amounts grew until 1997. Opinion polls, even those taken in the years immediately after the 1983 amend-ments, persistently reflected public skepticism about the system's longevity, and more and more media and academic attention fo-cused on the fact that on a straight taxes-paid to benefits-received basis, the system's rates of return were falling and projected shortly to reach negative levels for high-income workers. A num-ber of studies showed that eventually even average wage earners would receive "real" rates of return of only 1 or 2 percent (less than the rate achievable with federal bonds). In addition, there was greater attention and concern about the long-range outlook for federal entitlement spending overall. Seventy-five-year medi-care projections began appearing in administration testimony and publications in the mid-1980s, and various government and aca-demic entities began projecting how the demographic trends build-ing for the future would impact federal entitlements, as well as the overall federal budget, notably taking into account a growing and long-lasting federal debt burden.

"Entitlements" became the new buzzword for long-range fiscal policy concerns. The idea that entitlements could someday devour all other governmental functions because of their fiscal demands buttressed the growing concerns about the inadequate long-range financing pictures emerging for social security and medicare. Although action to constrain them was relatively muted, discourse over entitlements consumed much of the floor debates in omnibus budget legislation enacted in 1993 and 1997.[44] In between, there was a commission to examine the long-range entitlement issue and a Social Security Advisory Council to examine social security's long-range deficit. Both failed at their missions to garner a consensus on reforms, but by a wide margin, both concluded that action was needed soon to address the problems.[45] In contrast, another more independent commission, formed in 1998 under the auspices of the Washington-based Center for Strategic and International Studies, also examined the social security problem and was able to form a consensus around a major plan that incorporated the creation of mandatory and voluntary personal retirement accounts, part of which would be funded with existing social security taxes, and a complex set of large reductions in future social security benefits. With a composition including members of Congress of both parties and a wide range of business representatives and pension policy experts, its plan was provocative and added some depth and definition to the dimensions of change to which some policymakers were willing to ascribe.[46]

In summary, the social security problem has been persistent and served as a forerunner of major concerns about the fiscal demands that federal entitlements overall may pose in the future. Over the past 26 years, the social security trustees have reported that the system was insolvent—that is, not in "close actuarial balance"— 20 times. Twice, various administrations and congresses stepped in and made major changes. Nonetheless, the problems, or perceptions thereof, persist. Since the last major changes were made in 1983, 12 consecutive trustees' reports, through the terms of two presidents, have forecasted a significant long-range actuarial imbalance.

The reason the problem has been so resilient is complex and multifaceted. However, to suggest that it emanates exclusively from the failure of estimators to adequately foresee future trends and events is too simple. In hindsight, remedies employed in the past were incomplete. Lawmakers either deliberately left a discernible problem, as in 1977, or failed to address the problem with a hedge for uncertainties. Had they, for instance, looked at the projected year-to-year stream of income and outgo resulting from their proposed changes in 1983, it would have been evident that an "average" 75-year deficit would re-emerge very soon.

More significant though than the failure of past remedies to effectively match income and outgo is the absence of measures that inspire trust—trust that the changes made will build future resources. The projected future claim of entitlements on government resources overall dictates more than a narrow policymaking focus on social security's needs. It shows that even a cushioned and effective matching of projected income and outgo may not secure the resources that social security needs when all the other fiscal demands on the government come to a head 30 years from now. Policymakers can dictate today what they think social security's future tax and benefit rates should be, but whether those changes are sustainable has more to do with how future workers feel about the overall level of federal taxes they must bear. Thus, among the many reasons for the social security problem's resiliency is the perception, right or wrong, that as a nation we have not taken steps to assure that we are "saving" to meet it.

# CHAPTER 3

# The Case for Insolvency— How Seriously Do We Take the Projections?

Someone once said that the only thing certain about long-range social security projections is that they will be wrong. This may be true, but it does not diminish the need to make them. However imprecise or uncertain they may be, they are a vital tool of policy-making. No major company can survive without forecasts of its revenues and costs; why would presidents and members of Congress not consider them in trying to set a course for social security, a program with an inherent long-term focus? To make social security changes, or refrain from doing so, without making projections would be to make policy in a vacuum, and doing that would be grossly irresponsible, however weak and uncertain the projections may be.

## PUTTING THE PROJECTIONS IN CONTEXT

With rare if any exception, the conventional congressional perception of the adequacy or inadequacy of social security's financing has its origins in the pronouncements made by the social security trustees, whose forecasts and conclusions rest heavily on the work of the Social Security Administration's actuaries. It is not that the trustees and actuaries have employed the best projection methods—conservative critics have long asserted a fundamental flaw in their approach and have been frustrated for decades with their underlying "pay as you go" concept of measurement.[47] Their pre-eminence stems more from their long tenure and the precedents they have set for evaluating the system. There have been 60 annual trustees' reports issued over the life of the program; the actuaries' estimates have provided the basis for each of them and every reform made to the system since its inception. No other entity, public or private, has developed the same depth of expertise.

Formulating demographic projections from their own systems and the work of the Census Bureau, and using economic data from the earnings histories of social security taxpayers and forecasts of independent blue-chip economists and those of each administration, the social security actuaries have made life-long work out of evaluating the financial condition of the system.

Because they are part of the executive branch, it is not uncommon for people to question whether their projections are biased in favor of the sitting administration's policies and positions. Ultimately, they report to the commissioner of social security, who is in fact a political appointee, so when their projections support a particular political argument or an administration policy or proposal, it is easy to be skeptical. However, they are career civil servants whose hiring and job tenure rests not on their political affiliation but on their professional credentials. In addition, they have standards imposed by their profession, over and above those of rank and file civil servants, as well as a long history of serving the congressional committees of jurisdiction on a nonpartisan basis. They have, in a sense, a stake in maintaining an aura of objectivity. If their judgment and operating principles were called into question too often, their credibility would fall, credibility that to a large extent has not diminished over decades of service to policymakers of both parties. Moreover, the law requires them to certify the assumptions underlying the trustees' projections both as to their reasonableness and consistency with actuarial standards and procedures. Perhaps equally important as an insulating factor, the chief actuary cannot be removed from office without cause. Thus, to be skeptical of the trustees' and actuaries' projections, given the uncertainty of what they are asked to forecast, is reasonable; to suspect innate bias is largely unfounded.

The point of all this is not to mount a defense of the actuaries' work but to put their projections in context.[48] When there is contention over their forecasts (or changes thereto) or their reluctance to make estimates, it frequently stems from a sort of mystical view of their abilities. The layperson's expectation is often too high. *"Why don't they project economic cycles—forecast recessions and boom times? Why don't they show a growing immigration trend? Why is their fertility assumption for 2040 so low? Why do their longevity improvements decline over time?"*

There is no crystal ball in making social security projections. So much is contingent on demographic and economic conditions that haven't yet taken place. If the best forecasters on Wall Street can't predict a recession 2 years from now, why is it that we expect the actuaries to foresee economic and demographic conditions 25 years from now, and with precision? Was it in their power in 1955 to predict that the post–World War II baby boom would end 10 years later? Is it in their power today to foresee a potential 10-year improvement in average human life spans 20 years from now? A lot of the frustration with social security projections is based on unreasonable expectations about what the actuaries can do.

Many who are new to the social security debate instinctively question the projections. For those with an agenda, it is almost too easy. Because the assumptions reflect broad manifestations of society's behavior and because the future is unknowable, a reasonable alternative can be rationalized with almost every major category of assumption. When someone is trying to espouse a policy change, what better mechanism than an actuarial forecast of the policy's likely success—the thinking being that "if the actuaries would only use the *proper* assumptions, it will show that the policy will work."

Over the years, attacks of social security projections have come from both the "right" and the "left," as policy pundits attempt to show the truth to all who will listen. They also make great *op ed* pieces. Their downside, however, is that they distract policymakers. On tough policy calls, it is sometimes easier for policymakers to attack the messenger—in this case, the social security trustees and actuaries—rather than to address head on the issues they raise. To the credit of the Clinton administration and other administrations over the past quarter century, they have to a large extent resisted temptations to minimize or downplay the long-range social security problem.[49]

## DESPITE THE CONSIDERABLE UNCERTAINTY, THERE ARE DISCERNIBLE PATTERNS

But even setting political concerns aside, how seriously is one to take social security projections given their duration and uncertainty? The actuaries have no greater ability than other forecasters to observe the future. No one has the capacity to foresee social and economic conditions prevailing 20, 30, or 70 years from now. Congress and administration policymakers have always needed something around which to form policy, and the trustees and actuaries have given them that. But their projections are not highly reliable prognoses; they are simply "best guesses" and "best judgments."

At the same time, they aren't whimsical. They are built on current economic and demographic trends that in some instances have evolved over 30 or more years. The actuaries track these trends and build upon them to extrapolate projections. They are sometimes criticized for their conservatism, in holding to assumptions that appear inconsistent with recent trends.[50] However, what critics often fail to appreciate is that substantive trends emerge over a lengthy period of time. The difficulty and nagging question that any "trend-based" estimator confronts is "are the most recent phenomena a flash in the pan or truly discernible shifts for society?"

For social security purposes, among the most significant trends of the past 30 years are the decline in the nation's birth rate and the slowdown in "real" growth in worker's wages. From a baby boom peak of approximately 3.7 births per woman in her lifetime in 1957, the nation's birth rate fell to a low of 1.7 in 1976.

It subsequently rose to a little more than 2.0 in 1990, where it has now held for a decade. At this level, there would be zero population growth in the future. Lower levels would imply a reduction in population. In any event, the number of new workers to support the system would decline relative to the mounting retirement rolls.

### DOWNWARD TREND IN BIRTH RATES AND UPWARD TREND IN LIFE EXPECTANCY

| Year | Fertility rate (births per woman) | Life expectancy at age 65 (in years) | |
| --- | --- | --- | --- |
| | | Male | Female |
| 1940 | 2.23 | 11.9 | 13.4 |
| 1950 | 3.03 | 12.8 | 15.1 |
| 1960 | 3.61 | 12.9 | 15.9 |
| 1975 | 1.77 | 13.7 | 18.0 |
| 1990 | 2.07 | 15.0 | 19.0 |
| 2000 | 2.05 | 15.9 | 19.2 |
| 2025 & thereafter | 1.95 | 19.9 (in 2075) | 22.7 (in 2075) |

Intermediate assumptions of 2000 trustees' report

The ultimate long-range assumption under the trustees' "best guess" forecast is that the birth rate will decline gradually to 1.95 by 2025, where it will hold indefinitely.

Real wages, which had grown on average by 2 to 3 percent annually in the early postwar decades, hit a low point in 1980, when they fell by 6.7 percent (i.e., there was an average real wage *loss*). They moved up and down erratically over the subsequent 20 years, but on average they gained about 1 percent per year.[51] Under the trustees' current forecast, they are projected ultimately to rise by 1 percent per year.

### DOWNWARD TREND IN "REAL WAGE" GROWTH

| Period | Annual increase (in percent) |
| --- | --- |
| 1950–59 | 2.5 |
| 1960–64 | 2.1 |
| 1965–69 | 2.0 |
| 1970–74 | 0.2 |
| 1975–79 | 0.6 |
| 1980–89 | 0.5 |
| 1990–96 | 0.5 |
| 1997–99 | 3.6 |
| 2000–04 | 1.2 |
| 2005 & thereafter | 1.0 |

SSA and intermediate assumptions of 2000 trustees' report

The downward patterns in these assumptions didn't suddenly appear in the actuaries' work. They emerged slowly as current and past trustees modified their outlook year after year. They didn't emerge over any single administration's term of office, either— they developed over a period transcending six different administrations—both Republican and Democratic—going back to the Nixon years. The trustees do regularly reflect alternative forecasts with both lower and higher ultimate birth rates and real-wage growth patterns, but with the exception of the optimistic real-wage case, they typically don't come near the levels prevailing in the 20- to 25-year period following World War II. In the latest trustees' report, under the low birth-rate case, the ultimate rate is 1.7 births per woman (which is equal to the low point of the birth "dearth" during the 1970s), and under the high birth-rate case, 2.2. In the low real-wage case, the ultimate increase is assumed to be 0.7 percent per year, and in the high growth case, 2.4 percent. The important point about the trustees' three forecasts is that although differing in magnitude, they all reflect higher ultimate costs even when noticeably varying from the pattern set by trends in key assumptions.

Under the intermediate forecast, the social security trust funds would be expected to build up reserves until 2024, at which point they would be at their projected peak with $6 trillion in government securities recorded to them. They would then be drawn down (the result of the system's outgo exceeding its income) until they were totally exhausted in 2037.[52] At that point, social security tax revenues would be sufficient to pay only 72 percent of the projected benefits, and the system would be considered technically insolvent (i.e., the full amount of the payments prescribed by the benefit rules in the law would not be payable with the resources on hand). The cost of the system would rise from about 10.3 percent of payroll today to 19.5 percent in 2075, and for the 75-year period, on average its expenditures would exceed its income by 14 percent.[53] By the year 2075, the income shortfall would be 46 percent.

Although these estimates imply that social security can be kept solvent for the next 36 years, the system's taxes would begin lagging its expenditures in 2015. At that point, it would be relying in part on the government's general revenues, amounts owed to it in the form of interest payments. By 2025, interest payments and social security tax revenues together would no longer be sufficient to match the outgo, and the system would have to draw on its reserves. As these reserves consist exclusively of treasury bonds, by 2025, $1 out of every $5 of the program's outgo would be dependent upon payments from the general fund (i.e., interest and reserve redemptions combined). Expressed as an equivalent portion of today's annual expenditures, these claims would total more than $80 billion per year.

Certainly the problem as portrayed by these projections is significant. Nonetheless, they are just projections—reasoned and educated, but no less speculative about the future. Even a 15-year outlook is an incomprehensible horizon for some. Social security doesn't have an immediate problem, no benefit payments are threatened in the near term, and even if one considers the potential general fund draw in 2015 an issue, it won't be the first time that it has happened. The system went through a decade or more of making such draws in the 1970s and early 1980s. That said, are current policymakers really going to feel compelled to act on the possibility of insolvency 36 years away?

Those who tend to dismiss the projections generally focus on the long-run economic variables. In particular, they criticize the trustees' "best guess" assumptions about gross domestic product (GDP), which they feel are much too conservative. For nearly a decade now, real GDP has risen annually by 3.5 to 4 percent. In the last four years, it has averaged more than 4 percent, levels that are consistent with earlier expansion periods of the past half century. The trustees, on the other hand, project that the GDP growth rate will fall gradually to a level of 1.7 percent in 2020 and to 1.5 percent by 2075.

What's misleading about this discussion, however, is that the actuaries really don't build their social security forecasts directly from GDP projections. It is just the opposite; the GDP forecasts are simply derivatives of independent projections of labor force growth rates, wages, productivity, prices, and so on—the economic factors that most directly affect social security projections.

Because the long-range projections reflect a slowdown in the growth of the population (due to the last quarter century's decline in birth rates and the continuing low rates assumed for the future), eventually they reflect a slowdown in the growth of the labor force. Coupled with a lower assumed rate of real wage growth (again, based on the trend of the last quarter century), the two factors (albeit with others) lead to a slower growing GDP.

Some still question the scenario because of their belief in the potential of the so-called "new economy," that there is a long-term technological burst in productivity emerging. They believe that the robust GDP growth of the last few years is just the beginning, and because the actuaries and trustees rely so heavily on long-term trends, their current forecasts fail to reflect the rise in productivity and real wages that is looming.

Others, however, who focus on the demographic variables, raise concerns that the actuaries are not adequately reflecting potential improvements in longevity. If they were to do so, the system's long-range outlook would worsen as people would be expected to be on the benefit rolls for longer periods. The actuaries' projections do reflect continuing improvements in longevity, but at a gradually slowing rate. Critics take the view that there are numerous major gains in lowering mortality and morbidity looming from biotechnological advancements and breakthroughs in genetic sciences. They criticize the actuaries for not assuming a continuance of at least the rate of improvement that has been achieved in recent decades.[54]

## VARIOUS FACTORS BEG PRUDENCE

The debate about the validity of the actuaries' assumptions is exhausting and endless, and whether policymakers are better informed by it is questionable. How seriously policymakers should take social security projections is a judgment call. Should they view the future with a sense of optimism and the hope that these adverse projections can be overcome, or should they approach the next few decades with caution and prudence because of what they imply?

Although maybe not compelling, the factors begging prudence are substantial.

First, although social security's problem is often compared to a pig being swallowed by a python, it's not a good analogy.[55] It suggests that once the baby boomers pass away, the increased costs and potential strains confronting the system will diminish. This, however, is not what the projections show. With the retirement of the baby boomers, the system's costs rise, but they don't dissipate later. What happens is that the aging of society manifests itself sharply with the baby boomers' retirement and then takes on a sustained presence in the years that follow. Where there were 5 people of working age for every person age 65 and older in 1980, there are projected to be only 3.1 in 2025, 2.7 in 2050, and 2.4 in 2075.[56] The point is that the retirement of the baby boomers is not the central demographic event at issue; it is the aging of society generally. Although many things could change, the baby boom is a phenomenon that has occurred, the subsequent birth dearth is an event that is continuing, and improvements in life expectancy have not abated. With these factors in place, it is difficult to see how anyone can reasonably conclude that the demographic elements contributing to the adverse social security outlook are a temporary phenomenon.

Second, the point of departure in assessing the social security projections allows no room on the negative side. Unlike the debate that President Clinton and the 106th Congress engaged in about near-term fiscal policy choices and the possible uses of the present social security surpluses, there is no social security surplus to guard in the long run. Policymakers are starting with projections of deficits. However reasonable the hypotheses are for more favorable circumstances, they are only speculation. The deficits could also turn out to be larger. Is it realistic then for the baby boom generation to plan for its retirement with today's "best guess" being that social security deficits will emerge half way through? What if a more favorable scenario doesn't materialize? What is there to fall back on? There wouldn't be any trust fund reserves. Should the government impose higher taxes or reduce benefits? Under the current projections, a 28 percent benefit reduction would have to occur abruptly in 2037 if nothing were done before-hand, or if taxes were to rise, the increase would have to be nearly 40 percent. Where's the cushion?

Third, it is not just a social security issue confronting policy-makers. To the extent society's aging means that other entitlement programs will grow, they too will put pressure on federal re-sources, with constraints perhaps being imposed on every other "nonentitlement" activity of the government. If not, taxes may have to rise to unprecedented levels. Federal entitlement spending, now hovering at about 11 percent of GDP and representing more than half of all federal spending, could rise by two-thirds or per-haps double in the next 30 or 40 years, principally because of social security, medicare, and medicaid commitments. Federal dis-cretionary spending has ranged from 6.5 to 9 percent of GDP dur-ing the past decade and between 10 and 12 percent through much of the earlier postwar period. What is it about the future that leads us to think it will shrink as time passes? Why will future lawmak-ers want to cut the one segment of federal spending they can make choices about—that's not automatically spent by decisions made by their predecessors?

Even assuming that federal interest costs were erased by retire-ment of the government's outstanding debt, the cost of govern-ment in the aggregate could easily climb to 25 or 30 percent of GDP 30 or 40 years into the future. Through most of the last half century, it hovered around 20 percent, with the highest level being 23.5 percent in FY1983. Federal tax receipts, on the other hand, have rarely exceeded 19 percent of GDP, a level that some perceive as an implicit or natural barrier. How reasonable is it then to con-clude that future lawmakers will increase taxes to match the po-tential claims that future entitlements will impose?

Fourth, the experience with social security projections is not an encouraging one. Until very recently, the estimates tended to deteriorate over time, with the condition of the system worsening as new estimates were made. This has been the pattern for nearly 25 years and was certainly the case following passage of the 1977 and 1983 changes to the system. Although major improvement or long-range "actuarial balance" was projected to result from these changes, subsequent trustees' reports routinely showed a deteriorating picture in which the projected deficit grew larger and/or the point of "insolvency" came closer. Even though reports since 1997—when the trustees showed the largest average 75-year deficit since passage of the 1983 changes—have reflected some improvement, it has been small and mostly attributable to short-run economic conditions—conditions that could easily dissolve with a recession. The ultimate long-range situation hasn't changed at all.[57] Moreover, there is the adverse element built into each new trustees' report of adding a deficit year at the back end of the 75-year period and subtracting a surplus year from the front end. Thus, delaying action in the hope of a turn-around in forecast trends is, at least at this point, a tenuous strategy at best.

Fifth, there is the looming political reality of an aging society. It is one thing for politicians to take action today to resolve a future problem that may be overstated, and thereby create unexpected future surpluses. That's a "boon" for future politicians. It is an entirely different matter for them to understate or obfuscate the problem, leaving its resolution to those holding office at some later time. Today's demographics—the impending baby boomers' retirement in particular—don't bode well for the latter strategy. The elderly vote, and the 77-million-strong baby boomers will have a substantial vested interest in the status quo.

Finally, as each year passes, the time frame in which constraints to the system can be imposed gradually gets smaller. Thus, to the extent constraints are deemed necessary at some point, the longer policymakers wait to enact them, the more precipitous they may have to be.

A 25-YEAR PATTERN OF ADVERSE SOCIAL SECURITY FORECASTS

| Year of trustees' forecast | Shortfall of income (75-year average), in percent | Projected year of insolvency (trust funds depleted) |
|---|---|---|
| 1976 | 72.6 | Early 1980s |
| 1977 | 74.6 | Early 1980s |
| 1978 | 11.5 | 2028 |
| 1979 | 9.9 | 2032 |
| 1980 | 12.4 | 1983 |
| 1981 | 14.9 | 1982 |
| 1982 | 14.8 | 1983 |
| 1983 | None | — |
| 1984 | 0.4 | — |
| 1985 | 3.2 | 2049 |
| 1986 | 3.4 | 2051 |
| 1987 | 4.8 | 2051 |
| 1988 | 4.5 | 2048 |
| 1989 | 5.4 | 2046 |
| 1990 | 7.0 | 2043 |
| 1991 | 8.2 | 2041 |
| 1992 | 11.2 | 2036 |
| 1993 | 11.1 | 2036 |
| 1994 | 16.1 | 2029 |
| 1995 | 16.4 | 2030 |
| 1996 | 16.4 | 2029 |
| 1997 | 16.7 | 2029 |
| 1998 | 16.3 | 2032 |
| 1999 | 15.3 | 2034 |
| 2000 | 14.0 | 2037 |

Social security trustees' reports, 1976–2000

# Potential First Steps—Allocating Budget Surpluses and Defining a Role for Individual Accounts

Recognizing that the looming federal budget surpluses offer potential resources around which to at least start a dialogue, and that both political parties have pledged to reserve more than half of the surpluses pending action to reform social security, a fundamental question is deciding on a fiscal policy course for the intermediate-term future, the next 10 to 20 years. What are we going to do with the budget surpluses? How much will go toward tax cuts, how much toward spending, how much toward debt reduction, and how much toward addressing social security and medicare issues?

## DECIDING WHAT USE TO MAKE OF BUDGET SURPLUSES AND HOW MUCH TO CREDIT TO THE SOCIAL SECURITY TRUST FUNDS ARE TWO DIFFERENT THINGS

In the absence of any policy changes, some $1.1 trillion of the $4.6 trillion in projected federal budget surpluses over the next 10 years will be credited to the social security trust funds as excess social security tax receipts. The trust funds would receive credit for these excess taxes plus another $1.3 trillion in interest due from the government on their holdings of federal bonds—a total of $2.4 trillion. The government wouldn't actually use cash to make these payments. It certainly wouldn't receive any interest from some outside entity, and none would be needed. The Treasury Department would simply credit the trust funds with more federal bonds. In other words, deciding how to use the budget surpluses and deciding how much to credit to social security are not necessarily contingent on one another.

Although the expectation upon enactment of the Social Security Act in 1935 was that excess payroll taxes would be used by the Treasury to keep the federal debt lower than it otherwise would be—to sell fewer or buy up outstanding federal securities held by the public—it wasn't long before they were put to other uses. World War II emerged, ballooning the federal debt and soaking up every excess dollar of federal taxes, whatever their intended purpose. Excess social security taxes have been collected for decades since then, and the social security trust funds have been fully credited for them, but for most of the period, the government ran overall deficits. It used the social security money for something else.

The point here is only that defining how much of the budget surpluses to use for social security reform and deciding how much to credit to the social security trust funds are potentially two different things. The entire amount, for instance, could be redirected toward new individual savings accounts while crediting the social security trust funds for the full amount of payroll taxes received. Likewise, the same amount could go toward debt reduction while fully crediting the trust funds. Thus, while Congress has presumably set aside $2.4 trillion of the next 10 years' projected surpluses "pending" social security reform, that amount sets neither a limit nor a minimum on how it will allocate the aggregate surplus receipts among its various fiscal policy options.

## DECIDING HOW TO CREATE INDIVIDUAL ACCOUNTS IS BOTH AN OBSTACLE AND UNIFYING FACTOR FOR REFORM

Next, although both parties recognize a role for new individual savings accounts, whether and how such accounts might be part of a social security reform plan is a critical issue. The Clinton administration initially gave the impression that its so-called "universal savings accounts," proposed in early 1999, might be part of its social security reform package. However, it later tried to separate the issues, claiming that the new accounts were really part of private pension reform, an attempt to help extend and broaden coverage. The administration made the same claim in offering a considerably scaled-down version in the president's February 2000 budget submission to Congress. The not-so-subtle message was that such accounts were not negotiable within the context of shoring up social security.

The reality of the situation is that whether the creation of individual accounts is considered part of or separate from social security reform, it is part of an effort to shore up retirement planning and expectations—to shore up the nation's retirement income system in the aggregate. The posturing of the accounts as something separate from social security has more to do with a philosophical aversion to considering them as a substitute for social security. It is a way of saying that they have no place in a social insurance setting. It says that if the nation's social insurance system has financing problems, the formation of individual accounts should have nothing to do with their resolution.

It also makes little difference in a governmental cash-flow sense whether the surplus funds used to fund individual accounts are charged against the general fund or the trust funds; the amount of money diverted from the Treasury would be the same. From a social security policymaking perspective, however, it has a great deal of meaning. If the diversion is considered a charge against the general fund—that is, uses revenues "other" than social security's—the contributions that the government makes to the individual accounts would be considered something paid in addition to social security taxes, or what is referred to as an "add on" approach. On the other hand, if it is considered a charge against the trust funds, it would be considered using existing social security taxes, or what is referred to as a "carve out" approach.

For the system's defenders, the carve out approach is the most offensive of the potential arrangements. Although the amount of money diverted from the Treasury is no different in either case, the carve out approach diverts financing from the ledgers of the current social security system and, in an accounting sense, weakens an already inadequately financed system. For every percentage point of the social security tax rate diverted to an individual account, the system's average long-range cost has to drop by 6.5 percent. Thus, a 2 percent carve out would mean that on average benefits would have to decline by 13 percent from prescribed current law levels—a decline over and above the 28 to 30 percent decline that might be required because of the long-range income shortfall already projected.

The alternative of not diverting taxes from the system—in an accounting sense, by using general fund receipts instead—is less threatening. The amount of budget surpluses diverted may be no different than under a carve out plan, but the social security trust funds would be unaffected. They would be credited as they always have been, and thus the revenue diversion would have no bearing on their perceived long-range condition.

Also threatening, but in a much more subtle way, are individual account proposals where the eventual annuities paid from the accounts would offset (or pay for) part or all of social security benefits. Unlike the carve out approach, the social security tax base would be unaffected, and the system's benefit package would be the same for all practical purposes (albeit, now funded through a mix of public and private funds). However, the adoption of individual accounts interacting with social security would be viewed as a foot in the door for conservative reformers. It would be seen as a symbolic step toward eroding support for the existing system. Even the technical characterization of such plans—"clawbacks"— carries a menacing tone. Thus, for the system's defenders, signing on may be a considerable risk.

Finally, there is the strategy of formulating an individual account system having no effect on social security while simultaneously formulating measures to shore up the system. Neither social security's tax base nor its benefit package would be affected by the formulation of individual accounts, but other measures would be adopted separately to shore up the system. In principle, the policy choices for each would be considered independently from one another. In reality, however, that is unlikely to happen. Lawmakers would tend to view them as offsetting measures, even though the individual account accumulations would have no direct bearing on the size of each person's social security benefits (the annuities from the accounts would not offset the benefits). For instance, negotiating over the size of social security constraints would be driven by perceptions of how large a contribution to individual accounts would be acceptable (the larger it is, presumably, the larger the annuities would be and thus the larger the social security constraints could be). Consequently, even this strategy is likely to appear threatening to the system's defenders.

The one potentially unifying factor is that the creation of individual accounts offers a potential sweetener to whatever package of painful choices lawmakers may feel compelled to make. The real policy options for addressing social security's long-range shortfall are painful ones—enacting more taxes and benefit constraints. It's hard to imagine either party choosing only that course. By the same token, choosing only to make general fund infusions would do little to instill long-term confidence and by itself is unlikely to be acceptable to Republicans (and perhaps a significant share of Democrats). Thus, it may be that the critical first step in moving a reform plan forward is deciding if and in what form and size new individual accounts are to be created.

# CHAPTER 5

# The Painful Choices—What May Work, What May Not

The options policymakers have for resolving social security's financial imbalance break down into three generic choices: increasing revenue, constraining outgo, or borrowing. Because the projected elevated costs of social security are not temporary, borrowing would appear to be little more than a placebo. The baby boomers' retirement will cause the system's expenditures and those of other entitlement programs to rise to a higher plateau. There is no later time when the costs would drop off. Hence, if borrowing were the preferred course, the question arises of how long the government would be expected to borrow.

If nothing else, it is hard to imagine how proposing borrowing would be reassuring to an already skeptical public. After decades of running budget deficits and finally reaching the point where some or all of the government's debt can be eliminated, the public would be told that we can now borrow our way around a permanent elevation of entitlement costs. How meaningful could that be?

Crediting the trust funds with general fund "paper" sends a similar message. It is not an action that directly addresses the imbalance of receipts and expenditures. The Clinton administration's proposal to follow such a course was rationalized by assumptions that lower interest costs and constrained discretionary spending would free up future resources to offset the higher entitlement spending. The fact is, however, that discretionary spending, as its title implies, is not something that is easily controlled or limited by any rhetorical commitment made today. Its growth has not really abated, and relying on the resolve of future lawmakers to ignore perennial demands for government intervention is more wishful thinking than a sustainable plan for resource reallocations of the dimension involved. There is no real means to impose discretionary spending constraints on future lawmakers. Lowering or eliminating interest costs does offer some potential relief but in and of itself is not likely to be large enough to offset the potential entitlement bulge. And it too depends on a commitment of future lawmakers—in this case, to debt reduction.

The real choices for resolving the system's problems don't rely on assumptions, expectations, or implied commitments about what future lawmakers can or may do. They require current lawmakers to raise revenue or cut spending—to change the law now to explicitly raise future taxes or constrain future benefits. Raising future tax rates is certainly a substantive option, but it ignores or dismisses the looming fiscal demands of social security and other entitlements. Levying higher taxes today on future generations is tantamount to making the judgment that the higher tax burden will be acceptable to them. In an economic sense, society may be in a position then and of the mind to absorb the higher cost—the nation's GDP would be so much larger, even if only the trustees'

### THE TRUSTEES' "BEST GUESS" SOCIAL SECURITY FORECAST

| Year | Income | Outgo (as percent of taxable payroll) | Annual surplus or deficit (−) |
|------|--------|--------------------------------------|-------------------------------|
| 2000 | 12.65 | 10.34 | 2.31 |
| 2010 | 12.74 | 11.55 | 1.18 |
| 2020 | 12.91 | 14.66 | −1.75 |
| 2030 | 13.08 | 17.35 | −4.26 |
| 2050 | 13.21 | 17.96 | −4.76 |
| 2070 | 13.32 | 19.24 | −5.92 |

2000 trustees' report, intermediate forecast

"best guess" assumptions held. But there is no guarantee. We are nearly 2.5 times wealthier today as a society than we were in 1960, but in the years since, the federal tax burden has hovered narrowly in the range of 17 to 18 percent of GDP.[58] Future generations may be able to afford higher taxes, but they may not want to, and that could set up an untenable political situation. What if the tax increases are challenged as they take effect? Will we be able then to abruptly constrain entitlement spending? Will those already receiving benefits or who are close to eligibility age just sit back contentedly accepting large cuts? Are we not setting up future policymakers with a potentially intractable dilemma? How could they cut benefits once people were receiving them? The individuals wouldn't have time to adjust; they'd already be in retirement.

Simply stated, raising taxes ignores the fact that higher future entitlement costs could be a political burden, even if not an economic one. It may be that future generations will see a need to sustain the higher costs. But it should be their choice, not the consequence of the wishful thinking and obfuscation of an earlier generation. It, too, is much like borrowing, borrowing on the future earnings of today's children.

This said, taking prudent action today to reduce the future rate of growth of entitlements is probably the most contentious in a political sense. It does not increase the relative claim on the production and resources of future workers, and if today's assumptions about future entitlement demands prove to be pessimistic, there would be a "windfall" for future politicians to use—it would be easier to unexpectedly raise benefits for their constituents than to take them away. But its downside is that constraining future benefits today is easy to demagogue and requires policymakers to subscribe to the premise that there is no free lunch.

It is not unprecedented, however. The 1983 social security amendments did not make popular changes. Yes, at least at that point, the aggregate package did appear to restore the system's solvency, but the changes that made it so were not painless—the age for full retirement benefits was set to increase from 65 to 67, benefits were made partially taxable for income tax purposes for the first time, and COLAs were delayed almost immediately. Given today's political climate, the fact that all were accepted and still remain in force could be viewed as an awesome political feat. As Senator Moynihan often stated at the time, enacting those changes was foremost a showing that lawmakers could still govern. Perhaps most significant in that regard was a forced vote on the House floor that required members to choose between raising future taxes or raising the social security retirement age. Their decision was to raise the retirement age. In retrospect, the fact that they had put themselves in that position is fairly remarkable.[59]

What made that package workable? Certainly once the Greenspan Commission's recommendations were made, the political climate became far less contentious with both the administration and congressional leaders standing equally behind them. And the commission itself gave political cover to rank and file members. The proposals it made were not traceable to either party—they emanated from a blue-ribbon bipartisan body. Congressional leaders on both sides argued that while their members could find substantive parts of the package to object to, to chip away at it would be its undoing. The fragile agreement would fall apart. In the end, the strategy worked, and the package moved through Congress with considerable speed. From the announcement of the commission's recommendations on January 20, 1983, to achievement of a conference agreement between the House and Senate on March 24, 1983, only 63 days elapsed. President Reagan signed the bill into law on April 20, 1983.

The obvious lesson is that the "hard medicine" was worked out *in advance* by a small body of influential leaders, including members of Congress who were or could represent their party's leaders and administration officials who could negotiate for the president. It was not the use of a commission per se but that there was an effective medium for frank deliberations and negotiations.

Another lesson was that the ultimate measures enacted were not precipitous in their effects. The age for full social security benefits was set to rise from 65 to 67, but it wasn't to take effect for 17 years, and even then it was to be phased in over 22 years—a 39-year period from enactment to full effect. Equally important was that the first age of potential retirement was not altered. Workers could receive benefits as early as age 62, as under the old law, albeit with more of a reduction than before. That greater reduction too would be phased in over 22 years. The introduction of the income taxation of social security benefits also was done slowly. Income levels below which no tax would be required were set so high that only 8 percent of the recipient population was initially affected. Only those single persons with incomes above $25,000 ($32,000 for couples) would be affected, and only to the extent that their incomes exceeded those levels. By holding these exempt amounts constant, the measure was designed to phase in over time. As workers subsequently retired with higher aggregate incomes, a rising proportion would have some of their benefits taxed. Today, more than 30 percent of social security recipients are affected, but it took 17 years to get to this level. Even the required participation of federal workers in the system was done with restraint. Only new hires were to be mandatorily covered. Existing workers were not forced to join. Thus, initially only those not yet having a stake in the old civil service system were affected. Today, more than half of all federal workers pay into social security.

In effect, the measures taken, for the most part, were reasoned and tempered. With the exception of a small minority of relatively well-off recipients whose benefits would become partially taxable, no one on the rolls would see their immediate benefits reduced, and no one about to retire would see their expected benefits curtailed. The changes were hardly popular, but they weren't precipitous; their effects were shared in a generational sense (both current and future generations were asked to take less); and they were balanced enough to be acceptable to a Republican White House and both Republican and Democratic congressional leaders.

## WHAT THEN ARE THE HARD CHOICES TODAY?

From a practical standpoint, it's nearly a soothsayer's exercise to prognosticate about what proposals would fly or sink today. Political attitudes and the context in which decisions are made shift quickly. Proposals can lie dormant for years, only to surface and be enacted as circumstances change, memories of prior clashes fade, and unfavorable sentiments recede. As an example, there were a number of congressional resolutions passed in the years immediately preceding enactment of the 1983 changes pledging that social security benefits would never become taxable for income tax purposes. In the end, when presented as part of a multifaceted reform package, benefits were made taxable.

## PAYROLL TAX INCREASES?

In today's political setting, are payroll tax increases out of the question? With both parties espousing the desirability for some or a lot of general tax relief in the current Congress, it's difficult to imagine tax increases being part of social security reform. Even the system's hardened liberal defenders worry about their effect, particularly on the already shrunken rates of return projected for today's workers. But the populist message of "taxing the rich" has always had powerful appeal with respect to social security taxes, given that the taxes have never been levied on all earned income. In 2001, the tax rate on workers of 6.2 percent applies to earnings only up to $80,400.[60] Only about 6 percent of workers have earnings above this level, but some 15 percent of aggregate covered earnings in the economy are not taxed because of it. Hence, raising the taxable maximum is not off the radar screen. How large and as part of what kind of package would make the idea palatable is arguable, but to discount its prospects out of hand because it's a tax increase is to ignore its latent public appeal.

## BENEFITS CONSTRAINTS?

What would work on the expenditure side may be less obvious. The idea that as people live longer lives they should be expected to work longer has had considerable academic appeal, especially among actuaries, economists, and demographers. The notion that the proportion of one's lifetime spent in retirement should not necessarily grow as life spans increase comes across as eminently reasonable, given the longevity improvements that have occurred since social security's inception and the projected continuance of such in the future. A male reaching age 65 in 1940 had a projected remaining lifetime of 11.9 years; a woman, 13.4. By 2000, those figures had risen to 15.8 and 19.1. In 2050, they are projected to be 18.6 and 21.5.[61] In other words, ignoring economic factors and the benefit improvements made to social security over the years, a man retiring at age 65 in 2050 is projected to receive 18 percent more benefits over his lifetime than his counterpart retiring today and 56 percent more than his counterpart in 1940—simply because he has a longer life span. For a woman, the figures are 13 percent and 60 percent, respectively.

For the public, however, the idea of extending social security's retirement age may have considerably less appeal. First, it "reduces" future promised benefits. Second, it implies that people should work longer. Workers in the trades, in arduous jobs, and on assembly lines are not likely to be enamored with the prospect of waiting longer to reap the benefits of many years of demanding, time-card driven work. For many older workers, with various degrees of infirmities, there may be a need to slow the pace down. To suggest to them that they should work longer because people 60 years ago lived shorter lives doesn't cut it. Thus, labor unions, in particular, may find it particularly difficult to warm up to the idea. Telling their rank and file, notably those already in the latter parts of their careers, that they have to put in more time would be a hard sell.

Some policymakers have suggested that only the age for full benefits be raised, leaving the first age of eligibility at 62 (60 for widows). In effect, what would change is the amount of reduction a worker must take for retiring early. The current extension of the full benefit age to 67 actually works this way. When completely phased in in 2022, people retiring at age 62 will receive a 30 percent reduction for *retiring early*, in contrast to the little more than 20 percent reduction for someone doing so this year. It is in effect a benefit reduction because the only thing that will really change is the level of benefits payable at any given retirement age. Nonetheless, it has a similar ring to saying you have to work longer. For the layperson, it may only be a subtle distinction to say you need to work longer to receive full benefits than to get them at all.

Although the idea of using budget surpluses to create new individual retirement accounts has been percolating on Capitol Hill for a number of years, the concept of linking them to the resolution of social security's long-range deficit was given a considerable boost by economists Martin Feldstein and Andrew Samwick, who in a number of academic papers and op ed pieces suggested that annuities payable from such accounts might be a basis for a partial reduction in social security benefits—for example, for every dollar of annuity paid, there would be a $.50 or $.75 reduction in a retiree's benefits.[62] The idea they presented was not only that social security's financing problems could be resolved without tax increases or benefit cuts, but also future retirees could be made better off than if they received only their promised social security benefits—the combined individual account annuity and "offset" social security benefits would be higher. Their proposal was novel and became a catalyst for a number of bills and related proposals made by various members of the 106th Congress. It is incorporated in concept in the Archer-Shaw plan discussed earlier, one proposed by Senator Phil Gramm, bills by Representatives Mark Sanford and Nick Smith, and a number of others.

Although like other proposals to create individual accounts, decisions about how to use the budget surpluses and the form and size of the individual accounts need to be addressed; the idea that American workers could get larger benefits from a social security rescue plan lacking tax increases or benefit constraints has to be taken seriously. When viewed against the alternative of using the surpluses for tax cuts, the proposal is not free. Translated, foregone tax cuts are higher taxes. However, lawmakers do *not* have to pass a law to create the higher taxes, and from that perspective, the surpluses do provide a free lunch.

Despite its potential appeal, the proposal is not an easy sell. From the liberal side, it represents a threat, a foot in the door toward eroding the social insurance nature of social security. The feeling is that once established, people may come to prefer individual accounts over social security and question the program's underlying purpose. The proposal's opponents also will make many policy and technical arguments (e.g., social security's solvency will rest on the volatile stock market; the proposal is simply backdoor general fund financing; it's inefficient to set up millions of individual accounts; the proposal benefits the rich, etc.), but at its core, their opposition will emanate from fear that once lawmakers embark down this path, they won't be able to turn back.

The idea also suffers from a perceptual weakness: regardless of how it is packaged as a policy option, it is an *offset* proposal. People will lose money—that is, social security benefits—because they've grown personal savings accounts. One of the most stubborn constituent issues to plague members of Congress over the years has been the social security "earnings" or "retirement" test. Under it, retirees lose money because they continue to be gainfully employed. Their social security benefits are reduced or totally withheld if their earnings exceed certain levels. After decades of complaints, and numerous incremental liberalizations, the 106th Congress eliminated the test for nearly 10 million recipients between the ages of 65 and 69.[63] Whether the original arguments for its existence remain valid or not (foremost being that social security is not supposed to pay someone for just reaching a given age, but that it *replaces* lost earnings), the fact that its repeal was unanimously passed by recorded votes in both chambers of Congress shows the overwhelming appeal of its demise. The public felt it was being punished for working.

The so-called government pension offset is another example. Designed to reduce double dipping by government workers who have government pensions but claim to be dependent on someone with social security coverage, the measure is a constant source of friction between members of Congress and retirees in their districts. Social security affords dependent spouses with benefits to supplement those received by their covered husbands and wives. However, workers in governmental jobs, who don't pay into social security and aren't covered, receive pensions of their own from their government work. They often aren't dependent on their spouses but attempt to claim a social security dependent's benefit. Many don't get it (or get greatly reduced amounts) because their social security benefits are *offset* by their government pensions, and they complain vigorously that they are being singled out as government workers. Again, whether the basis and arguments for the provision are well founded is not the point—retirees don't easily accept offset measures.

Although there is strong political appeal for lawmakers to be able to tell the public that they will be better off having individual accounts that partially offset social security, the question arises about whether it is a sustainable policy. Are future retirees going to accept a benefit offset for growing the accounts? If they truly are individual accounts that give workers a greater sense of ownership and investment flexibility than social security, are future retirees going to be passive about losing benefits because of their success at building these nest eggs? Are retirees 20 years from now going to remember that this helped rescue the social security system from insolvency? Are they going to feel better off? Better off than what? Than they would have been if the law hadn't been changed many years earlier? Why should they be any more accepting then than today's retirees have been of the social security earnings test?

In effect, the problem with the proposal is that future retirees would be told that because they saved in their individual accounts, they would lose something. If they didn't lose something, there wouldn't be any savings to the social security system. On a political level, it is an idea that's initially appealing. However, in practical terms, it is like other government efficiency measures; it takes something away. In this case, people would lose benefits if they were successful investors—the greater their success, the more they would lose. Thus, at some point the public would likely protest, and if Congress later acquiesced, the system could be threatened again.

A similar issue arises with the idea of means-testing social security benefits. Under means testing, not long ago suggested by the Concord Coalition,[64] a recipient's income and assets would help determine how much benefits they would receive. Presumably, social security benefits would be computed as they are under current law, but once determined they would be subject to reduction if a recipient's total income or assets were above certain levels. If taken literally, it implies periodically measuring a person's income and net worth before certifying their benefits. Although initially enticing as a policy option, limiting whatever pain must be borne to those most able to take it, it has a number of major hurdles to overcome.

First, it runs counter to the essence of social security. Workers are supposed to feel they've earned their benefits by working and contributing to the system. Social security is not supposed to be a welfare payment. The benefits aren't supposed to be a gift from the "people," something given because of a showing of *need*. Benefits are paid as an *earned right*. To condition them on a showing of low income and assets would transform the basic image on which the program was constructed. Moreover, the proposal has antisaving, antipension, and antiwork implications. Why should someone save or work if the marginal gain will be substantially eroded by losing benefits?

Then there is the issue of how the income and assets of some 45 million people would be measured and validated. What kind of entity would it take? No government welfare program today— federal, state, or local—gets anywhere near examining the economic condition of a population this large. And although potentially an administrative nightmare, how are recipients themselves going to feel about it? They've worked all their lives, paid into the system, and now have to justify how deserving they are by divulging their economic state to some anonymous government bureaucracy? Although there may be ways to shield a large segment of the population from a benefit loss, such as with high-income thresholds, the magnitude of social security's long-range problem is such that even middle-income recipients would have to be affected if sizeable savings were to be achieved.

The point here is that even setting philosophical issues aside, the problem with most benefit constraint measures is that they aren't straightforward. Their rationale, the way they achieve their savings, or their secondary implications are distracting. The list goes on. COLA cuts hurt the "old old," who suffer the highest poverty rates among the aged and have no means to adjust for the lost purchasing power of their benefits. Cutting dependents' benefits has a disproportionate impact on women. Lengthening the number of years over which earnings are averaged adversely affects the disabled, those who leave the labor force to raise children, and others with lengthy periods of unemployment.

## IS THERE A "STRAIGHTFORWARD" BENEFIT CONSTRAINT?

What the public clearly does not recognize is that the system's future benefit levels are preprogrammed to rise not only nominally but also in real value, across the board. They will do so automatically, and this rise contributes to the eventual imbalance between the system's projected income and outgo perhaps as much as the future growth in the number of its aged recipients. Why automatically? Under current law, the commissioner of the Social Security Administration is required to adjust the social security benefit formula annually for wage growth, the purpose being to keep initial benefits up with the real growth in the value of wages.[65] Wages tend to rise faster than prices over time, the difference being largely due to increases in productivity. For the most part, the difference represents the worker's share in the nation's real economic growth. As wages rise in the future in excess of inflation, so will the social security benefits of future retirees.

Simply stated, under the system's automatic adjustment features, the benefits it pays to future retirees will be worth more on a relative basis than those paid to today's retirees—they will be higher in real terms, meaning they will buy more. This is economic speak for saying that the role of the program in furnishing retirement income will not contract over time as the nation gets wealthier. If an average wage earner retiring at 65 today gets 42 percent of his or her preretirement earnings replaced by social security benefits, a wage-adjusted formula will give approximately the same rate to all future retirees. (The incremental rise in the full benefit age now in the law does dampen the amount of real growth, but the residual is still substantial.)

On the surface it may sound reasonable, but on closer examination it begs the question that as the nation gets wealthier, why does it have to rely so heavily on social security as a source of retirement income? Why does the government have to maintain as significant a role 30 years from now as it does today? Can't other means of saving for retirement take a larger role? In supplemental views, five members of the 1979 Social Security Advisory Council put it this way:

> As per capita income rises, the case for increasing the amount of mandatory "saving" for retirement and disability through social security is far weaker than was the rationale for establishing a basic retirement floor of retirement and disability protection at about the levels that exist today.
>
> At the levels of real income prevailing in the 1930s (or perhaps even the 1950s), it can well be argued that it was appropriate, indeed, highly desirable—perhaps even necessary for the preservation of our society—that government should, by law, have guaranteed to the aged and disabled and their dependents replacement incomes sufficient to avoid severe hardship, and to have required workers (and their employers) to finance this system with a kind of "forced saving" through payroll tax contributions. But as real incomes continue to rise, it is not easy to justify the requirement that workers and their employers "save" through payroll tax contributions to finance ever higher replacement incomes, far above those needed to avoid severe hardship. Perhaps not all workers will want to save that much, or to save in the particular time pattern and form detailed by present law; some may prefer to save in quite different time patterns, or in forms involving quite different tradeoffs between risk and probable return.[66]

Some also might ask that if the system has long-term problems, why should the real value of social security benefits be allowed to go up automatically? Why should the purchasing power of future retirees' benefits be increased when the tax burden on future workers has to rise so sharply to achieve such generosity?

The real rise in benefits can be tempered without raising the retirement age, offsetting benefits, or selectively reducing the system's generosity for one group or another. It simply requires enactment of a more moderate annual adjustment in computing future benefits. Benefits could still be allowed to rise for inflation—future retirees would not have to take lower benefits than their predecessors—but any real increase in value would be left to future generations to decide. It's not unprecedented to have benefits adjusted in such an ad hoc fashion. This was, in fact, the general practice for four decades after the program's inception. Or, alternatively, Congress could decide at some future date that it wanted the program to rise in real terms again in some automatic fashion.

The beauty of this approach is that it is an administratively simple constraint with a relatively even impact across all segments of the beneficiary population. Benefits would be computed in a manner similar to current law, but an adjustment would be made in the basic benefit computation to remove the real wage gain built in the annual formula changes made by the commissioner. Doing this would eliminate (or approximately so) the projected long-range deficit of the system without telling people to work longer and without offsetting or withholding benefits. And, most importantly, it gives future policymakers greater discretion.

Speaking in support of a similar approach that they recommended as a means of addressing the looming demographic shift, the aforementioned members of the 1979 advisory council argued that it was their

> judgment that future Congresses will be better equipped than today's Congress to determine the appropriate level and composition of benefits for future generations . . . Congress might elect to give more to certain groups of beneficiaries than to others, or to provide protection against new risks that now are uncovered. But precisely because we cannot now forecast what form those desirable adjustments might take, we feel the commitment to large increases in benefits and taxes implied under current law will deprive subsequent Congresses, who will be better informed about future needs and preferences, of needed flexibility to tailor social security to the needs and tastes of the generations to come.[67]

The problem with the proposal is that it strikes at the philosophic heart of the program. It says that it's "ok" to have social security's role contract in relative terms over time. For today's ardent believers in the social insurance concept, it would be caving in to the new reformers. By shrinking the relative role of the program, the government would be weakening not only the redistribution of income the program provides but also the bedrock benefits—the "safety net"—that social security provides in favor of forms of retirement income that are perceived, rightly or wrongly, as more volatile and less socially designed. Other programs, such as supplemental security income (SSI) and state-run cash assistance, would be expected to pick up more of the antipoverty goals of the system. Simply put, the proposal takes a large step toward a clearer delineation of the work-related retirement income and antipoverty functions of government. Those who subscribe to the social insurance approach would resist such a change. Unlike social security, the constituencies for welfare programs are not strong and vocal. Social security's advocates feel that the government would never adequately deal with poverty among the aged and disabled through welfare programs and that only through a hybrid program like the existing social security system—which creates a stake for middle- and upper-income workers—can poverty among these groups be effectively tempered.

## WHAT WILL MAKE PAINFUL CHOICES PALATABLE?

In whatever form, any future constraint on the social security system's expenditures has to appeal to the public on the basis that the system *needs* to trim its future commitments and with the perception that it is being done fairly. That has to be the ultimate message. Without it, it is hard to see how any sizeable benefit constraint would be palatable. If the policy debate is confined to the projected long-range imbalance of the trust funds, it may serve only to confuse the public. The trust funds are a set of governmental accounts. The projected imbalance between their income and outgo does reflect the long-range growth of social security expenditures, but not the potential strain on the government of meeting all of its expenditures. It is a significant but condensed view of the issue. The trust funds' imbalance, for instance, could be fixed on paper by merely crediting them with $3 trillion, give or take, in new federal securities.[68] No money would have to be raised or other expenditures cut. Congress could just pass a law requiring the Treasury Department to post the requisite securities to the funds. To the extent that this was put forth as a means of resolving the problem, the potential overall burden of social security and other entitlements would be obscured. It would be "passing the buck," so to speak, by simply making the problem an indefinite responsibility of the government's. It wouldn't help focus attention on the real issue—identifying how the elevated costs of government, and the accompanying tax burden, would be mitigated. It is only by nurturing an understanding of the potential magnitude of that burden that the public could begin to have an appreciation for the necessity to consider curtailment of the program's growth.

# CHAPTER 6

# Where There Might Be Fertile Ground

Among the most fascinating of political events is when conventional wisdom breaks down and the unthinkable reaches center stage. What particular alignment of political circumstances would be conducive to action on social security is hard to predict, but the gridlock on the issue in the 106th Congress does not necessarily dictate the script for the 107th. Seasoned Congress watchers know that no Congress can bind its successors. As with the stock market, where the time to buy is often favorable when pessimism prevails, so it is with many public policy issues. The seeds of compromise frequently emerge when the rhetorical conflict flares. Whether it's the desire to responsibly "govern," a questioning of one's conventional dogma, the persuasiveness of the opposition, or simply impatience with gridlock, the players least likely to see the world the same often come together when the prospects for such seem least likely.

Whether the public is ready now for some significant reform of social security is mostly a matter of conjecture. Social security is very much the public's program, and before anything substantive can happen, there needs to be an understanding and consensus about what the issues are. It is the role of political leaders to educate the nation about such issues and the various means to address them. Certainly President Clinton's elevation of the debate and the

2000 presidential campaign helped stimulate a closer look at the system, but concluding that the issues have smoldered long enough for the public to have formed some sense of if and how much to change the system is debatable.

If a serious effort at reform is to have legs, it won't come from the system's trustees, a study commission, a congressional committee of jurisdiction, or the "bully pulpit" of a president. It has to come from widespread public conviction that reform is needed. No significant changes to social security have ever been made without the leadership and support of a president, but all were accomplished only after acknowledgment from congressional leaders of their importance. And those leaders, in turn, have needed the agreement of their respective caucuses that the changes would be meaningful to the public.

## OPENING A POTENTIAL DIALOGUE

"Touching the third rail" may be politically dangerous, but to maintain that there is free lunch to be had is a prescription for entrenchment and further gridlock. The initial acknowledgment by both camps that politically difficult changes have to be made to put the existing system back into long-range balance is potentially the first step in opening a dialogue.

However, starting the dialogue from the standpoint that paying anything less than current law benefits is a "cut" may impede, more than help, the process. Fostering recognition that the system's benefits are preprogrammed to grow in "real" terms, and that this growth contributes to its financial imbalance, is a way of putting potential constraints in a more meaningful context. For the public, the conventional view of reducing future benefits is to make them less valuable than they are for today's retirees. In fact, under the trustees' latest wage and price increase assumptions, current law benefits are projected to grow by 25 percent in real terms by 2030 and by 67 percent by 2060 (albeit, recognizing that the latter will not be payable if the system's funding gap materializes). Thus, fostering an understanding that benefits could still grow or at least hold their value even if set at lower levels than scheduled under current law offers a way of approaching difficult choices without the prejudicial images of "benefit cuts."

Similarly important is the recognition of the potential role newly created individual accounts could play as a potential sweetener to balance off whatever politically difficult choices at which policymakers can arrive. Although future retirees may not get as much from social security as prescribed under current rules, they would be able to accumulate separate nest eggs to make up part or all of the difference—or even do better. Today's workers would own and control these supplemental retirement assets instead of relying on the government to levy higher future taxes, cut back on other future spending, or borrow to pay for the now unfunded social security benefits that are promised.

## RECOGNIZING EACH SIDE'S PHILOSOPHICAL LIMITS

What is most troubling to social security's liberal defenders is the direct linking of new individual accounts to the system, either by funding them through a diversion of social security taxes (i.e., carving them out) or where social security benefits would be offset (reduced or forfeited) by some or all of the annuities payable from the accounts (i.e., through the so-called clawback or other mechanism). For the system's liberal defenders, it is tantamount to replacing the existing system with a "privatized" one. Even in partial

### PROJECTED "REAL" INCREASE IN FUTURE SOCIAL SECURITY BENEFITS

| Year of retirement at age 65 | Initial monthly benefit (in constant 2000 dollars) | Increase in real value of benefit (in percent) |
|---|---|---|
| 2000 | $987 | — |
| 2010 | $1,098 | 11 |
| 2020 | $1,191 | 21 |
| 2030 | $1,233 | 25 |
| 2040 | $1,358 | 38 |
| 2050 | $1,495 | 51 |
| 2060 | $1,647 | 67 |

Computed using "intermediate" assumptions of 2000 social security trustees' report

form, it represents a foot in the door. Moreover, from their perspective, the carve out simply means there is more of a long-range
problem to solve, giving the public more to be skeptical about. It
doesn't help solve the problem; it aggravates it.[69]

Conservatives fear that if there is no direct linking, there will be
no social security changes. It would be too easy for lawmakers to
forego making changes, and the individual accounts would simply
become another government entitlement. Conservatives believe
that the way to force social security changes is to have the accounts
affect either the system's income or outgo streams, or both—only
that will open the door. They also believe that newly created individual accounts can survive the test of time only by giving the
workers who pay social security taxes a sense that it is their money
being used. That's why a carve out approach is so philosophically
important. Conservatives feel that without it, there can be no real
sense of ownership. They contend that accounts funded from general revenues would come to be viewed as governmental handouts
and eventually be minimalized or repealed altogether as lawmakers come to question their use against other spending priorities.
The carve out, on the other hand, represents giving people back
the taxes they paid and allowing them to save them on their own.

## A POSSIBLE LINCHPIN?

Setting aside, for a moment, the issue of whether the individual
accounts are created from general revenues or social security taxes,
the proposition that such accounts have a potential role in enhanc-
ing future retirement incomes and that projected excess governmental receipts—budget surpluses—offer a means of funding them
is accepted on both sides. This may in fact be the only thing offering common ground, but it also could become a linchpin for more
comprehensive action. The *direct* linking of the new accounts to
social security may be a line liberal defenders will not cross, but in
the absence of making a "fix" to the system, the enactment of
individual accounts could effectively become a gap filler for the
nearly 30 percent reduction in benefits implied under current law.
Stated more bluntly, gridlock on reaching a remedy to the system's

projected long-range deficit is implicitly a policy of eventually pay-ing lower benefits. In effect, regardless of whether liberal defenders accept or reject the idea of creating individual accounts as part of fixing social security, their union may be the practical outcome of developing them separately from social security reform.

This then begs the question of wouldn't it be preferable to de-velop an individual account system that was designed to make up for the constraints needed to close the funding gap? Why let the prospect of insolvency linger? Why let the idea fester that benefits might have to be reduced abruptly at some future point because of political gridlock? Why not design the new accounts and benefit constraints to mesh in some reasonable way? Inevitably, designing and enacting them separately is a prescription for capricious and uneven outcomes.

Most importantly for liberal defenders is that acting assertively in this way would limit, at least in a financial sense, the magnitude of change to be made to the existing system. It allows for much of the system's basic precepts to be left intact while eliminating its long-term deficit. Liberals could acknowledge a role for individual accounts funded with budget surpluses, but insist that the accounts not be charged against the trust funds. Thus, the carve out ap-proach would be off the table because it would worsen the trust funds' long-range deficit by definition. It also gives the liberal side an opportunity to develop individual accounts that by design carry forward some of the underlying social concepts of the existing sys-tem. Developing individual accounts and benefit constraints sepa-rately may lead lawmakers to be influenced by factors irrelevant to "social insurance," foremost being whether the accounts should be universal. The probability is great that they would otherwise be voluntary. Under such an arrangement, even with strong incentives to participate, many workers wouldn't. Social insurance princi-ples, however, would beg for universal coverage of all workers so as to lessen the likelihood of their impoverishment and depen-dency in old age. They also could argue for preclusion of pre-retirement withdrawals, provisions giving survivors and divorced spouses a stake in the accounts, limitations to discourage risky investments, possible performance guarantees, and mandatory periodic payments in lieu of lump-sum withdrawals.

For conservatives, it results in a reduction in the government's role in the provision of retirement income and gives individuals more responsibility, more choice, a greater sense of ownership, and potentially more rewards for the efforts they make. The value of their social security benefits (assuming these accounts were considered a part of the system) would not be conditioned solely on the willingness of future lawmakers to levy the taxes to pay them. In a short-term sense, it also allows for absorption of a portion of the budget surpluses for something other than growing government expenditures and in this way has many of the fiscal attributes of a tax cut. Although this would result in less debt reduction than current law, the economic effect would be little or no different. Under a debt reduction scenario, when the holder of a federal security is paid off, much of that money presumably flows into other financial assets. Diverting budget surpluses into individual accounts would do the same. For conservatives, however, diverting the money into individual accounts gives people more of a stake in how the budget surpluses are used. Lawmakers wanting to veer from a debt reduction course so that they can increase government spending might find it easier to do than if the same amount of money had been earmarked for individual accounts. No individual could point to a personal economic loss. However, lawmakers wanting to put less money into individual accounts would have to face their constituents, who are likely to protest the smaller contributions. Thus, for conservatives, this approach provides more assurance that at least a portion of the budget surpluses could not be used to expand the role of government.

The key for conservatives, however, is in defining people's stake in the accounts. If the carve out approach is off the table, what are the principles under which the accounts are to be funded? How are workers to be given a true sense of ownership if not through a reversion of their social security taxes back to them? Will liberals seek to tilt account deposits heavily toward the poor? Will they exclude people? After all, if the funds used are not someone's social security taxes, they are general revenues, and why should general revenues go toward funding personal accounts for the well-to-do?

One approach at compromise might be to fund the accounts by means of refundable tax credits. Social security taxes would be credited to the trust funds in the same fashion as they are today, but workers would be given a "tax credit" equal to a portion of them—say, two or three percentage points worth of the 12.4 percent overall rate (i.e., 16 to 24 percent of the taxes they and their employers pay). Hence, the social security trust funds would not be adversely affected as they would be under a carve out plan, but workers would be given some sense that the amount going into their accounts represents taxes they have already paid.

This approach would not be something new; it was done for workers and the self-employed for a period of time following passage of the 1983 social security amendments to mitigate the abruptness of tax hikes included in that law and is the ongoing means by which low-income workers are given regular relief from the social security taxes taken out of their pay through the so-called earned income tax credit (EITC). More importantly, it is not far from a regular practice employed for *all* workers under the tax code. The employer's share of social security taxes and all self-employment taxes are credited to the social security trust funds even though the employer's share and one-half of self-employment taxes are deductible for income tax purposes. The general fund absorbs the impact of the foregone income tax receipts. The use of a tax credit to fund the individual accounts could be viewed as a return of one or the other, or both, of two forms of "excess" taxes—social security or all other (the bulk of the latter being income taxes). Simply put, the dollars credited to their accounts would represent a return of taxes not needed by the government today, but by their mandatory set aside and investment, they would permit future taxes to be lower than they might otherwise have to be.

This approach is not without its drawbacks, however. First, it may very well come across as "backdoor" general fund financing of social security. As such, for conservatives it could raise the specter of opening a wedge toward uncontrolled program expansions, and for liberals it may be seen as a first step toward means testing. Second, to the extent policymakers continue to view budget surpluses as having two parts, with that which is attributable to social security being off the table, the tax credits would then likely have to be charged against the general fund. It therefore would put the creation of the accounts in competition with all other possible uses of the notably smaller "on budget" surpluses and in so doing potentially constrain the amount available for individual accounts. The amount of overall resources perceived available to policymakers would be smaller because by default the social security portion would have been effectively set aside for debt reduction.

Nonetheless, it does provide a means to address the more fundamental concerns that each side has raised about the other's preferences. Moreover, on the surface, the system would continue to be financed with payroll taxes in the same manner as under current law, and the amount of general fund involvement would be clearly defined in the form of an explicit tax credit. Thus, the threat for conservatives of the open-ended nature of making non-earmarked general fund infusions would be lessened. And for liberals, the system's excess receipts would be earmarked for debt reduction, thereby preserving the system's tax base for future use and forcing the newly created individual accounts to compete for other possible uses of on-budget surpluses.

## HOW THEN TO CONSTRAIN THE EXISTING SYSTEM?

This then leaves the question of what constraint options to consider in attempting to fix the existing system. One obvious course is to look at the multitude of congressional plans introduced in the past few Congresses. At a minimum, they represent approaches that some lawmakers have been willing to offer and debate publicly. The problem, however, is that many are comprised of a complex array of provisions. Only with expert insight could most lay people begin to understand how they work and what elements are most significant. In effect, these plans already reflect the churning of the congressional process, in that as they have gathered co-sponsors or anticipated interest or advocacy group criticism, elements were added, others removed, and still more were modified. Some plans are simply a smorgasbord of social security cuts or revenue measures drawn from a laundry list of actuarial estimates of generic options. How or whether they fit together as part of a single bill is hard to decipher. Even when accompanied by estimates of their long-range impact on the social security trust funds, the impact on future benefit levels and/or retirement incomes is hard to comprehend. The authors frequently choose benefit examples that show the best side of their plans, and many plans are incomplete.

Adding to the confusion is that many plans include carve out provisions such that the proposed social security benefit reductions are much larger than they need to be if designed only to close the long-range funding gap. The carve out provision creates a larger hole to fill, and thus the constraint measures included in the plans are larger in impact. Still others contain both carve outs and provisions permitting voluntary contributions, which further complicate any attempt to decipher how exactly a person would fare from each element of the bill.

Simply put, many of the congressional plans thus far introduced are as confusing as they are insightful as displays of the potential means to constrain the growth of the existing social security system.

## THE FOUR PROMINENT CONSTRAINT OPTIONS

If one looks hard at the congressional plans, the substantive constraint approaches they encompass consist of four basic options:

- Raising the retirement age
- Offsetting benefits by some or all of individual account annuities or payments
- Cutting back on the size of automatic cost of living adjustments (COLAs)
- Constraining automatic growth adjustments to the benefit formula and procedures

## Raising the Retirement Age

The idea of raising the social security retirement age probably has received the most attention and is incorporated in one form or another in a number of bills in the last three or four Congresses. Some, like current law, would only raise the "full" benefit age, whereas others would raise the age for "first receipt" as well. Some would have these age thresholds rise gradually to certain new fixed levels, say 65 for first receipt of benefits and 70 for full benefits. Others would raise them indefinitely in tandem with increases in longevity. As people live longer, their social security benefits would start later and be adjusted accordingly.

The iterations of "age-related" proposals are numerous. Without question, many would make a major dent in the program's long-range deficit, if not completely eliminate it. And, as previously described, the rationale for making them is strong. However, with the principal perception of them being that people will be required to work longer before benefits can be paid, the message such plans send is distracting. Coupled with mediocre public support, particularly from those in union-backed occupations, the likelihood that any form of the idea will run into stiff resistance is great.

## Offsetting Benefits for Individual Accounts

Proposals to offset benefits to reflect some or all of the annuities or periodic payments from growing individual accounts also have potential to produce significant program savings. If both political camps took the idea seriously, it could generate a considerable following if for no other reason than it might be a means to preserve the level of benefits promised under current law. The problem with the idea, however, is that it would take very large offsets—for instance, nearly 100 percent of the annuities projected under the Archer-Shaw plan—to achieve enough savings to claim that the proposal by itself would resolve the system's problems. Moreover, it would likely suffer from the chronic problem of being perceived as taking away something that was earned.

## Cutting COLAs

COLA constraints received considerable attention in the 1980s, when the budget deficits were large, and again in the mid-1990s, when the Bureau of Labor Statistics and other economists reported that the consumer price index—the measure used to calculate the COLAs—was possibly overstating the rate of inflation. Since then, many of the technical issues with the index have been addressed by changes the bureau has made, and inflation itself has remained low. Moreover, to have a sizeable impact on the system's long-range deficit, a COLA limit would have to take effect almost immediately and stay in effect for decades—year after year "diet" COLAs. Thus, the obvious and most significant political issue cutting COLAs raises is that it impacts the current recipient population in probably the most visible way possible. In the past, proposed COLA constraints have been easy targets for advocacy groups, particularly when census studies show that those most likely to be seriously disadvantaged are the "old old," who suffer very high poverty rates. Hence, the idea has limited potential from having both an outdated rationale and a likely political battering from its perceived punitive impact on those least able to absorb it.

## Constraining Future Benefit Growth

Removing the automatic "real" growth in future benefit levels by constraining the annual adjustments made to the benefit computation procedures is probably the easiest to portray without distraction. It serves no purpose but to slow the growth of benefits for future recipients and, like the other approaches, could result in substantial savings, possibly of sufficient magnitude to eliminate the entire long-range problem. Its theme may be more appealing than the others as well—benefits would be lower than scheduled under current law, but the floor of income protection afforded by the system would be approximately the same as it is for today's recipients. In other words, savings would arise from precluding benefits for future recipients from growing beyond what is necessary to keep their purchasing power constant from one cohort to the next. Nonetheless, as with the other possible constraints to the system, it does represent a scaling back of the role of the program and thus would be perceived and potentially represented as a threat by the program's staunch defenders.

## WHAT THEN WILL FLY?

From this author's perspective, the combination of universal individual accounts, funded by government tax credits charged against the general fund, and a measure to constrain the automatic indexing in the benefit formula and computation rules to remove the element of "real" growth in the value of future benefits offers the best hope for common ground. Its rationale is simple and direct, and its impact is uniform across the recipient population.[70, 71] However, whether this approach is really preferable to pairing individual accounts with any other form of social security constraint is speculative at best. From a legislative perspective, any proposal to pay social security benefits lower than those afforded under the current rules is unappealing. There is no such option around which social security proponents can be expected to rally. None may be acceptable, and all can be challenged.

Substantive reform will come if and when elected leaders give it a nod, when all corners say they have talked and heard enough about the issues and that it's time to come to the table. The question of what will fly then becomes relevant. President Clinton and congressional leaders came close to that point in late 1998, but not close enough to move the process forward. The Clinton proposal did not address the issues enough to be considered a serious effort at engagement.

What exactly would it take?

First, a reasoned attempt at compromise, something beyond the lure of a free lunch. Proposing general revenues, albeit even in an era when excesses exist, as the fundamental element of reform does little to address the underlying fiscal issues and even less to bolster public sentiment. To also maintain that debt reduction is the prescription is to suggest that all future fiscal policy decisions can first be subjected to a social security litmus test: *Will these decisions impair debt reduction and thus harm social security?*

Debt reduction may come across as sound economic theory, but suggesting that future presidents and Congresses will subscribe to such a test before making all other taxing and spending decisions bangs heads with political reality. What if there is a war . . . a recession . . . some cataclysmic event . . . some yet undefined major call for governmental intervention in the economic or social affairs of the nation? Why is it reasonable to believe that future lawmakers will ignore all other calls for governmental action to achieve debt reduction? And what happens when there is no debt to eliminate? Why would social security be safer then? Its revenue and expenditure streams wouldn't have changed. The public may very well want to preserve social security in its current form, but it still needs a sense that the steps taken to do so are real.

If the system is to be made more secure, liberal defenders cannot put their head in the sand and insist that no constraints are warranted. To do so ignores the potential economic and political strain that the higher future cost of government could impose as a result of society's aging. Likewise, for conservative reformers to argue that individual accounts are the be all and end all, and can be substituted for social security to achieve the same social benefits, is to ignore the substantive differences in their approach. Even if they're right, they cannot insist on the wholesale dismantling of an institution that today keeps so many people out of poverty and for so many years has been an accepted cornerstone in assuring at least a minimal standard of living for the nation's elderly. In both camps, ideology needs to be subjugated to political practicality.

# Notes

1. In considering the original Social Security Act in 1935, the Senate passed an amendment by Senator Bennett Champ Clark of Missouri to the social security bill recommended by the Senate Finance Committee (H.R. 7260 of the 74th Congress) that would have exempted employees of firms with private pension systems from social security coverage. Related measures had been narrowly defeated in earlier committee deliberations. However, although passed by the Senate, the Clark amendment was dropped by conferees for the House and Senate who reconciled differences between the bills of the two bodies, and a subsequent attempt in the House to put it back in the bill failed. In 1950, with pressure mounting from the Truman administration to greatly expand the system, a pivotal decision was made with passage of H.R. 6000 to rely on the "social insurance," non-means tested approach embodied in social security in lieu of a "charity" or expanded welfare-type approach. Republicans at that time had preferred the latter, a universal system that would have paid flat-rate government benefits to all at age 65, but they got little more than a resolution to study the concept. Among the many changes subsequently enacted was an approximate 77 percent benefit increase, which helped to solidify the "social insurance" approach for the coming decades. See Martha Derthick, *Policy Making for Social Security* (The Brookings Institution, 1979).

2. The statutes under which social security taxes are authorized are entitled the *Federal Insurance Contributions Act* and the *Self-Employment Contributions Act*, FICA and SECA (they also authorize the medicare Hospital Insurance [HI] tax). However, payments made by workers to social security are by no means "contributions" in a voluntary sense.

They are taxes levied on the earnings of workers who are mandatorily covered by the program, and have always been treated as such.

3. One notable exception of recent years was an attempt by Senator Pat Moynihan in 1990 to make immediate reductions in payroll tax rates, followed by higher rates in later decades as the system's commitments increased. It was not so much a reaction to public disfavor with the system but a way of forcing a closer examination of the system's "surplus" funding, resulting from a rebounding economy and amendments made to social security in 1983, and how those largely unanticipated surpluses were being used in the allocation of resources under the federal budget process.

4. The Social Security Board of Trustees is made up of six members, who are largely politically appointed representatives of a sitting administration. Except for two who serve as representatives of the "public," most of the board serves for the duration of an administration's term. The board consists of the secretaries of Health and Human Services, Labor, and Treasury, the commissioner of social security, and the two public members appointed for four-year terms. The deputy commissioner of Social Security serves as secretary to the board. The board is required to report by April 1 of each year on the financial status of the system. Their report typically consists of short-term projections covering the following 10-year period and long-range projections extending 75 years into the future. One of the most frequently cited figures used in social security policymaking is the "average" 75-year balance between income and outgo under what the trustees' label their "intermediate" path. The intermediate path, discussed at length in this monograph, is comprised of assumptions that taken together represent the trustees' *best guess* about the factors that will influence the system's future financial flows. Although the trustees use various measures to express the financial health of the system, generally if the system's average outgo for the 75 years is projected to exceed its income by more than 5 percent, it is deemed to be out of actuarial balance—or in layman terms, *insolvent.* Since the inception of the program, there have been 60 trustees' reports issued. The last 12 reports have projected intermediate path shortfalls in excess of 5 percent (4 earlier ones also showed negative imbalances, but they were less than 5 percent). They have ranged from 5.38 percent in the 1989 report to 16.68 percent in the 1997 report. In the latest report issued on March 30, 2000, the figure was 13.99 percent for the period from 2000 to 2074.

5. They consisted of the Bipartisan Commission on Entitlement and Tax Reform (1995), the 1994–96 Quadrennial Advisory Council on Social Security (1997), the National Commission on Retirement Policy (1998), and the Social Security Advisory Board (1998).

6. The 1994–96 Social Security Advisory Council was the last of a multidecade series of legislatively mandated councils charged with examining and making recommendations about the program. Under the applicable law, a new council was formed every four years with broad representation from business, labor, policy experts, and the public at large. (A 1993 law separating the Social Security Administration from the Department of Health and Human Services repealed the provision calling for these quadrennial councils. In their place, a new permanent bipartisan advisory board was established.) The 13 members of each council typically were "newly" appointed each time the council was formed, although frequently members were given repeated appointments. The last council, which issued its report in January 1997, focused on the program's long-range financing problem and various ways to resolve it. They were unable to garner a consensus around a single plan but instead issued a report laying out three alternatives around which various factions of the council had coalesced. The so-called "maintain benefits" plan, endorsed by 6 of the 13 members, was the one favored by supporters of the current system. It attempted to address the long-range funding problem with the fewest possible changes. Principal among the changes suggested were an increase in the income taxation of social security benefits, a redirection of income taxes to the social security trust funds that now go to the Hospital Insurance (HI) portion of the medicare program, and an eventual payroll tax hike. The group also supported the idea of investing up to 40 percent of the trust funds' holdings in equities (in lieu of investing them exclusively in federal bonds), but shortly before issuing the report, they refrained from endorsing this. In the end, they only recommended that Congress consider the idea. In some respects, this plan appeared to be more of a reaction to the more reform-minded approaches suggested by the other two council factions, particularly by failing to propose a complete package of solvency measures. It represented a point of view that the problem was not as serious as the other factions made it out to be and that there were lots of small things that could be done to fix it. In contrast, 5 other members of the council advocated a complete redesign of the system (referred to as the "personal security account" plan) that would have gradually replaced the retirement portion of the current system with flat-rate benefits based on length of service and personal savings accounts funded with a 5 percent of pay contribution (carved out of the current payroll tax). The new accounts were to take the form of a "defined contribution" system, closely resembling IRAs or other individually based retirement vehicles through which participants build their own nest eggs directly. Taken together, the two elements of this plan would have phased out much of the social insurance nature of the current system. It would have covered the costs of transitioning to

the new system with a 1.52 percent of pay increase in payroll taxes and government borrowing. The third alternative (referred to as the "individual account" plan), recommended by the council chairman and one other member, addressed the funding problem mostly with gradually growing benefit reductions. They viewed the system as eventually being unsustainable when its aggregate financing burden swelled with the retirement of the baby boom generation and took the position that the system's role in the provision of retirement income needed to be constrained. To make up for some or all of the lost benefits, they would have required all workers to make a 1.6 percent of pay contribution to new personal savings accounts over and above the existing social security taxes they pay. Many observers saw this third plan as a compromise between the other two.

7. The term "entitlement" as used here differs from the legal concept of a "contractual" right. An entitlement afforded by the federal government is a benefit prescribed or dictated by federal statute. The government, however, is not bound to adhere forever to that statute because Congress can pass a law to amend it. Literally speaking, a federal "entitlement" is not the result of an agreement in the conventional context of a contract, where there is a commitment between two parties—in this case, the government and workers covered by the social security system—that for a given amount of compensation from one party, something will be done for the other. Although social security is often described in political debates as a "contract" or "compact" between generations, within the strict meaning of the term, the premise that social security is *not* a contract has been tested and affirmed by the Supreme Court (Fleming v. Nestor, 363 U.S. 603, 1960).

8. The Republicans lost 26 seats in the House. Ann Lewis, director of the Democratic National Committee at the time, said after the election that Representative Claude Pepper, then a chairman of the House Select Committee on Aging, who repeatedly attacked Republicans for trying to cut social security benefits, was the most sought-after representative of the party by Democratic candidates. He reportedly made 70 appearances in 25 states on behalf of Democratic candidates. See "Pepper in Demand as National 'Symbol,' " *Congressional Quarterly*, November 6, 1982.

9. This action occurred in consideration of S. Con. Res. 32 of the 99th Congress, a required annual congressional resolution setting budget targets for the upcoming fiscal year. This one was for fiscal year 1986. Among a number of controversial votes was a tie-breaking, 50-49 vote on May 10, 1985, when the Senate adopted its Republican-led Budget Committee's recommendation to "freeze" COLAs in social security and various other federal entitlement programs for one year. Although not included in the final budget resolution agreed to with the House, it too became a symbol for Democrats of Republican efforts to cut social security benefits.

10. Eliminating the limitation on earnings for recipients at or above the full benefit age, as proposed, was estimated to raise short-term costs only, i.e., for the next couple of decades. It was not estimated to raise the system's long-term costs, i.e., over the next 75 years, largely because the receipt of benefits by many individuals at age 65 meant that they would not receive so-called delayed retirement credits, thereby producing savings in the later portion of the social security actuaries' projection period. Delayed retirement credits are benefit increments paid to workers who delay filing for benefits beyond the full benefit age—currently age 65. By accepting benefits at age 65, no delayed retirement credits would be paid. Improvement of the lot of aged widows, however, would carry both short- and long-term costs. One proposal endorsed by various factions of the 1994–96 Social Security Advisory Council and thought to be favored by the Clinton administration was to provide a surviving spouse with 75 percent of the combined benefits that the couple received when both members were still alive, if higher than the survivor benefit payable under current law. Under current law, a widow/er is eligible for his or her own retirement benefit (from his or her own work record) or an amount equal to the deceased spouse's predeath benefits. In many instances of two-earner couples, 75 percent of the combined predeath benefits would produce a larger survivor benefit than under current law.

11. In his State of the Union address on January 19, 1999, and his subsequent budget released in early February 1999, President Clinton outlined what the administration called a *framework* for dealing with social security's long-range financing issues, which the administration estimated would eliminate two-thirds of the system's average deficit. He proposed reserving 58 percent of an estimated $4.9 trillion in excess federal receipts for the next 15 years—some $2.8 trillion of budget surpluses—for social security. The proposal envisioned crediting this amount to the social security trust funds as a general fund infusion, with 79 percent being used to buy down outstanding publicly held federal debt and 21 percent being used to buy stock.

He subsequently made some revisions to the idea and announced a new plan on June 28, 1999, when raising his 15-year surplus projections from $4.9 trillion to $5.9 trillion. The new plan called for general fund infusions to the social security trust funds of $543 billion in the FY2011–2014 period, followed by an indefinite $189 billion annually thereafter. These amounts were presumably equal to the interest savings to the Treasury from using social security surpluses to reduce outstanding federal debt. In effect, they too would have been a form of "double crediting" because current practice already would have credited the trust funds twice a year for the interest due of its holdings of federal securities. The new infusions were to be invested in stocks until the stock portion of the overall trust fund holdings reached 15 percent. The Social Security Administration's actuaries projected that these infusions would delay the trust funds' insolvency from 2034 (as the trustees had projected in their 1999 report) to 2053.

On October 26, 1999, the administration transmitted draft legislation to Congress reflecting yet another plan. It resembled the June plan but omitted calling for investments in stock. It called instead for crediting the trust funds with $735.2 billion in federal securities in the FY2011–2015 period, followed by $215.5 billion annually until 2044. These amounts represented revised estimates of the interest savings from using social security surpluses to reduce outstanding federal debt. The plan was projected to extend the life of the system until 2050. It also called for earmarking one-third of "on-budget" surpluses for medicare reform and budget process changes similar to those being considered in Congress to discourage use of social security surpluses for other purposes.

In his State of the Union address on January 27, 2000, President Clinton continued to press for his plan; however, unlike his October 1999 proposal, this one again called for investment of part of these new infusions in stock. Some 50 percent of the infusions were to be invested in stocks until the stock portion of the trust funds' overall holdings reached 15 percent. In effect, this proposal was close to the one he recommended in June 1999. The new trust fund infusions were to begin in FY2011. The SSA actuaries estimated that they would range from $98.7 billion in FY2011 to $204.9 billion in 2016 and thereafter (with all such infusions ending in 2050) and that the plan would extend the life of the system until 2054.

12. President Clinton described the proposal as "earmarking" part of the budget surpluses expected for the next 15 years for the social security system. The actual excess tax dollars would be used to reduce the publicly held federal debt and would be credited to the social security system by recording an equivalent amount of government securities to its trust funds. The idea was to plant the notion that buying up the debt would be to the benefit of the social security system, thus creating a political "firewall," so to speak, against using the money for some other purpose than debt reduction. When details of the proposals later emerged, the social security system actually was to be credited with a given amount of general revenues based on projections of budget surpluses made in January 1999, whether or not the surpluses later emerged. In other words, although there was a rationale articulated for crediting more securities to the trust funds, in practice, if the measure had been put into the law, the amounts credited would not have been driven by the subsequent materialization of budget surpluses. Simply stated, there would be general fund credits given to the system regardless of the financial condition of the

government. According to a description prepared by SSA's deputy chief actuary, the amount of the general fund infusions were to be largely predetermined at the time of enactment and would become annual mandatory "payments" to be made to the trust funds during each of the following 15 years (Memorandum from Stephen C. Goss, deputy chief actuary, and Alice H. Wade to Harry C. Ballantyne, chief actuary. *Long Range Effects of the President's Proposal for Strengthening Social Security Information*, February 12, 1999).

13. One of the key weaknesses with this argument, however, which detracted from its credibility, is that a debt-reduction strategy adopted today would not necessarily bind future policymakers. Many lawmakers recognized that although shrinking the federal debt was clearly a priority for the 106th Congress, it might not be one for later Congresses. In effect, the proposal was conditioned heavily on the conviction of future lawmakers to "stay the course," as well as having a continuing robust economy such that the surpluses would materialize as projected.

14. The proposal, referred to as "The Social Security Guarantee Plan," was unveiled by its sponsors at a press conference on Capitol Hill on April 28, 1999.

15. They also pointed out that the assets in the personal account could be passed along to the estate in the case of workers who died before retirement and had no survivors eligible for social security benefits. Thus, the account assets could be passed along to grown children not otherwise eligible for social security survivor benefits and others having a claim on the estate. In other words, the plan did not call for complete forfeiture of account assets to the social security system.

16. In a number of unpublished memoranda shared with this author, the social security actuaries projected that the plan would effectively eliminate the system's average long-range deficit.

17. Among them were the Washington-based CATO Institute and Heritage Foundation (David E. Rosenbaum, "When Ideology Goes Where Actuaries Tread," *New York Times,* May 2, 1999). In a February 16, 2000, briefing paper, the CATO Institute argued that the plan could lead to another savings and loan–type crisis (Andrew G. Biggs, *The Archer-Shaw Social Security Plan, Laying the Groundwork for Another S&L Crisis*).

18. Among initial critics was the Center for Budget and Policy Priorities, a liberal-leaning Washington advocacy group, which argued in an April 28, 1999, white paper that the proposal had major financing shortcomings (that it would "inadequately" finance the system when budget surpluses were no longer available, that it was an "inefficient and wasteful" form of general revenue financing, that it could weaken support for the traditional "defined benefit" nature of social security, and in some

respects it was "inequitably" tilted toward upper income workers ("The Archer-Shaw Social Security Proposal," by Robert Greenstein). Some of these concerns were similarly echoed by Democratic Representatives Earl Pomeroy and Benjamin Cardin.

19. White House economic advisor Gene Sperling stated that President Clinton "*appreciated that Chairman Archer was putting forth a serious proposal . . . and that if we had criticisms of it, they would be done in a constructive manner*" (Associated Press, April 29, 1999).

20. In an interview printed in a recent Hoover Digest, Milton Friedman, for instance, is quoted as saying, "*The young have always paid for the social security of the old. But the young used to pay for the social security of their own parents. Now the young pay for the social security of somebody else's parents. That's a change for the worse—I think it is a very unjust system. . . . We want responsible individuals. People should take care of their own old age.*" Interview by Peter Robinson of Milton Friedman, *Hoover Digest,* no. 3, Hoover Institution, 2000.

21. Message to Congress, June 1934.

22. As quoted by historian Arthur Schlesinger, Jr., *The Coming of the New Deal* (Houghton Mifflin Co., Boston, 1959).

23. Although not a prominent view even among social security proponents, there are those who do question the validity of the trustees' long-range deficit forecast. Much of their criticism revolves around the trustees' economic assumptions, which they allege are too conservative. The basic thrust is that with stronger economic growth, the potential strains of the aging of society can be overcome. See for instance, Dean Baker and Mark Weisbrot, *Social Security: The Phony Crisis* (University of Chicago Press, 1999); and Phil Mullan, *The Imaginary Time Bomb* (IB Tauris, 2000). Also see Robert Friedland and Laura Summer, *Demography Is Not Destiny,* National Academy on an Aging Society (1999). New York actuary David Langer takes the view that the trustees' projections are so skewed to the pessimistic side that he questions the professionalism of the Social Security Administration's (SSA's) actuaries on whose analysis the trustees base their forecasts. Although unsuccessful in his bid to have the American Academy of Actuaries step into the fray, he attempted to have the academy conduct an independent review of the professional standards applicable to the work of the SSA actuaries. The academy did not do so, and in fact, through its own educational activities and literature appears to have taken the position that the public needs to be better informed about social security's long-range deficit.

24. Although the average actuarial imbalance of the system increased steadily following passage of the Social Security Amendments of 1983 up to 1997 (under the trustees' intermediate forecast), it declined in the subsequent three reports issued from 1998 to 2000. The imbalance

peaked in 1997 at an amount equal to 16.68 percent of the system's average 75-year income, and the trust funds were projected to be depleted in 2029. The imbalance in the trustees' March 30, 2000, report is estimated to be equal to 13.99 percent of the system's average income, and the point of trust fund depletion has moved back to 2037.

25. Note the reluctance of Vice President Gore to support the idea in his presidential campaign, even after proposed by President Clinton in his FY2000 and 2001 budgets.

26. Contrary to conventional wisdom, one of the primary causes of the deterioration in the system's long-range outlook since enactment of the alterations in 1983 was changes in "actuarial methods," i.e., refinements in the way the social security actuaries make their projections. This is not to suggest that the now different economic and demographic trends comprising the trustees' current forecast are not as significant as policymakers believe them to be, but only that a major factor and potential source of uncertainty in the projections is the complex data aggregation and techniques employed by the actuaries.

27. Congressional Budget Office, *The Budget and Economic Outlook: An Update*, July 2000. In determining the social security portion of the budget surpluses, the Congressional Budget Office and others assume that the annual surpluses projected for the trust funds are synonymous with social security's share of the budget surpluses. Assuming such, however, overstates the degree to which social security contributes to budget surpluses. Much of the annual surpluses recorded to the trust funds comes from interest "paid" by the government. Because such payments are internal transactions between Treasury accounts, they are not receipts for the government. If one counts only the projected *excess tax receipts* the government takes in for social security purposes, it results in a much lower share being attributable to social security—$1.1 trillion over the next 10 years instead of the $2.4 trillion shown by the Congressional Budget Office's figures. This is not to suggest that the system is not due the interest recorded to its trust funds, but only to make the point that more dollars have been set aside in the current budget debate than are justified by social security's cash-flow surplus. If one says that the government should be using surplus social security taxes to reduce its outstanding publicly held debt until social security changes are enacted, the amount now being set aside for this purpose is too large.

28. In reality, there is no way to trace the use of any excess "dedicated" taxes the government receives. Once social security or any other taxes reach the treasury, the money becomes fungible. It's a matter of convenience to budget observers to suggest that excess social security taxes automatically offset other government spending or, alternatively, reduce other government borrowing as is sometimes alleged. If either per-

spective is taken literally, as they often are, it suggests that fiscal policy-makers ignore social security in examining and making aggregate tax and spending decisions. In practice, presidents and members of Congress who are responsible for overall fiscal policy take the entire realm of government functions into account in determining the appropriate levels of taxes and spending born by and paid to the public. It is the overall condition of the government that helps shape its impact on the economy. On occasion in the past, when certain objections were raised about the high level of social security taxes, members of congressional tax-writing committees adopted provisions to offset the social security tax bite with adjustments and credits to individual or employer income taxes (e.g., consider the original motivation for the earned income tax credit). In other words, in the decisions that were made, excess social security taxes were being offset by reductions in other taxes—and were not used for new spending or to hold down publicly held debt. It is really a matter of conjecture, not fact, to say that all excess social security taxes have been used for other federal spending or as an alternative to keep the government's publicly held debt lower than it otherwise would be.

29. For budget presentation purposes and for various aspects of formulating and enforcing federal budget targets in Congress, social security and the postal service are considered "off budget." Everything else is considered to be "on budget." These rules evolved through various pieces of legislation enacted from 1983 to 1990. Although intended to change the overall "image" of the federal budget, it did not change any features or financing aspects of these programs, nor did it change what the government as a whole takes in or spends in any given period. It simply distinguished social security and the postal service from the other activities and functions of the government.

30. *Proposals Certified to Save Social Security*, hearings before the Committee on Ways and Means, U.S. Congress, House, June 9 and 10, 1999, Government Printing Office, Washington, D.C., 2000.

31. The 1970 trustees' report stated that an estimated 90 percent of the aged population was then eligible for benefits.

32. For instance, under the old "static" estimating methodology, i.e., prior to the enactment of automatic benefit increases and its accompanying automatic financing features, the projected cost of the program tended to be routinely overstated. The methodology generally showed average benefit levels rising while earnings in the economy were assumed to remain constant. The cost of the program would then be shown to grow as a percent of taxable payroll, and future tax rates would be set to meet that cost. Subsequent earnings in the economy, however, would tend to rise over time, leading to larger projected payroll tax receipts, rendering a "surplus" not reflected in the earlier trust fund projections.

33. Most significant among the changes was a decrease in the assumed annual average "real" wage gain. In the 1974 report, the long-range "real" wage gain was assumed to be 2 percent annually. In reports just a few years earlier, it had been as high as 2.9 percent. By 1980, the assumed rate had dropped to 1.75 percent, and in the latest report, it was assumed to be only 1 percent.

34. Inflation had only increased prices by 35 percent over the same period. See *1998 Green Book*, U.S. Congress, House, Committee on Ways and Means (Government Printing Office, Washington, D.C., 1998), p. 70.

35. Ibid., p. 27.

36. The projected average long-term deficit following enactment of the 1977 legislation was 1.46 percent of payroll for the 1977–2051 period, compared to the trustees' current estimate of 1.89 percent of payroll for the 2000–74 period.

37. See Senate Resolution No. 113, passed 96-0, *Congressional Record*, May 20, 1981.

38. For a more detailed overview of the conflict, see coverage of the "budget" and "social security" issues in the 1981 edition of the *Congressional Quarterly Almanac*.

39. The inter-fund borrowing authority permitted the temporary transfer of securities among the two social security trust funds—the Old Age and Survivors' Insurance (OASI) and Disability Insurance (DI) trust funds—and the medicare Hospital Insurance (HI) trust fund. The fund most in distress at the time was the OASI fund.

40. *Republicans and Social Security, Five Decades of Opposition.* Special Report No. 97-58, Democratic Study Group, October 10, 1982.

41. The *Report of the National Commission on Social Security Reform* was transmitted to the president and congressional leaders on January 20, 1983. Twelve of the commission's 15 members supported a consensus package that dealt with the short-run problem and also addressed two-thirds of the long-range problem—COLA delays, new coverage of federal government workers, and the partial income taxation of benefits were principal among its recommendations. Seven of the same 12 members supported resolving the remaining long-range problem with a gradual increase in the system's full benefit age, whereas the other 5 supported an increase in payroll taxes.

42. In 1983, the balances of the trust funds were projected to grow from their level then of $25 billion (including amounts borrowed from the medicare HI trust fund) to $245 billion by the beginning of 1993, representing a cushion of two-thirds of 1993 expenditures. They actually grew to $331 billion and represented nearly a full year's worth of expenditures.

43. Although it is sometimes asserted that Congress intended then to build large trust fund reserves to help the system meet its long-range commitments, this is more folklore than substance. The changes made were based on near-term pessimistic economic assumptions that antici-pated that barely enough reserves would be accumulated to carry the system through the remainder of the decade. Congress had no perception of the system's financial flows after the first 10 years, and with respect to the long run, only "average" 75-year estimates were prepared for com-mittee deliberations. There was no discussion of "advance funding" the system's commitments, and little or no appreciation for the fact that an early build up of reserves would occur.

44. *The Omnibus Budget Reconciliation Act of 1993* (P.L. 103-66), and *The Balanced Budget and Taxpayer Relief Acts of 1997* (public laws 105-33 and 105-34).

45. This 32-member *National Commission on Entitlement and Tax Reform* was created by an executive order of President Clinton's and was jointly chaired by Senators Bob Kerrey and John Danforth. The 13-member Social Security Advisory Council was mandated by law and headed by Edward Gramlich, then dean of the School of Public Policy at the University of Michigan and now a member of the Federal Reserve Board.

46. This privately formed 24-member National Commission on Re-tirement Policy was led by six co-chairs, including four members of Con-gress—Senators Judd Gregg and John Breaux and Representatives Jim Kolbe and Charles Stenholm.

47. The criticism typically stems from the fact that social security's financial health is not evaluated on the same basis as a private pension. Private pensions are required to advance fund their future obligations. Private pensions are "deferred compensation," setting aside and invest-ing funds as the compensation is accrued to cover their future pensions. Thus, each generation is required to provide the resources for its own retirement. Social security, on the other hand, has been financed on a pay as you go basis for much of its history. As such, it passes most of each generation's benefit cost on to future generations. The difference in ap-proach largely stems from the fact that Congress has the right under the Constitution to alter taxes and spending unilaterally for the benefit of the nation. Unlike private pensions, social security's benefit package is not a contractual obligation—it and the taxes that support the program can be altered from time to time as Congress sees the need to adjust them. A company may go out of business, but with full funding of its pension plan, worker's benefits are protected at least as accrued to that point. The government, on the other hand, is unlikely to go out of business, or if it were to, preserving social security would be among the least of the

nation's problems. Thus, the trustees generally have taken the position that if the system's projected income is sufficient to cover its projected outgo on a current basis, its financial condition is secure.

48. In fact, this author has his own concerns about the organizational placement of the Office of the Actuary. The actuaries are under the direction of the commissioner of social security, yet they are required to certify the reasonableness of assumptions adopted by the system's trustees, of whom the commissioner is now one. The "certification" requirement was enacted prior to Congress making the commissioner a trustee. Although the chief actuary's independence is buttressed by his being removable "only for cause," the fact that he has to "certify" the reasonableness of key assumptions made by his "agency head" leaves at least a question about the practical independence of his office.

49. In this regard, it is interesting to note that although the long-run problem is smaller in the latest trustees' report than in reports of the preceding few years, it is still higher than the level reported when President Clinton took office. The average 75-year deficit reported in the 1993 trustees' report was 1.46 percent of payroll. In the latest report, it was 1.89 percent of payroll.

50. See, for instance, *The 1999 Technical Panel on Assumptions and Methods*, a report prepared for the Social Security Advisory Board, November 1999.

51. See 2000 Trustees' Report, loc. cit.

52. The trustees estimate that the Disability Insurance trust fund would be exhausted in 2023 and the Old Age and Survivors' Insurance trust fund in 2039. It is on a combined basis that the two trust funds would be exhausted in 2037.

53. For purposes of comparison, the cost rises to nearly 14 percent of payroll in 2075 under the optimistic forecast, but there is an average 75-year income surplus of 3 percent. In contrast, under the pessimistic forecast, the cost rises to more than 28 percent of payroll in 2075, and there is an average 75-year income shortfall of 37 percent.

54. See again the report of *The 1999 Technical Panel on Assumptions and Methods*, loc. cit.

55. For instance, see Paul Krug, "Reckonings, The Pig in the Python," *New York Times,* June 21, 2000, p. A27.

56. 2000 trustees' report, loc. cit.

57. In the 1997 report, the system average 75-year cost was projected to exceed its average income by 16.7 percent. In the latest report, the comparable figure is 14 percent. In the earlier report, the system's cost was projected to climb to 19.18 percent of payroll in 2070; in the latest report, it would climb a bit higher, to 19.24 percent of payroll. In both reports, the shortfall between income and outgo in that year would be 44 percent.

58. Real GDP rose almost fourfold over the period and is nearly 2.5 times higher on a real per capita basis. See *Economic Report of the President* (U.S. Government Printing Office, 2000).

59. It might be noted that the 1977 amendments made even deeper cuts in the projected future benefits of the system. Unlike the 1983 amendments, however, there was little contest over the need to make those changes; the debate was more about how deep to cut than about whether major constraints were needed. Even then, with the House, Senate, and White House all under the control of the Democratic Party, the debate was not intense. Republicans did offer an alternative plan to those being pushed through each chamber, but they did not garner enough votes to mount a serious debate.

60. This is the tax rate paid by employees and employers, each, for a combined rate of 12.4 percent. When the medicare Hospital Insurance tax is added on, the rate rises to 7.65 percent on each for a combined rate of 15.3 percent. In contrast to the social security portion of the overall rate, the medicare portion is levied on all earned income—there is no annual limit.

61. See 2000 social security trustees' report, loc. cit.

62. For one of their most recent papers of the subject, see Martin Feldstein and Andrew Samwick, *Allocating Payroll Tax Revenue to Personal Retirement Accounts to Maintain Social Security Benefits and the Payroll Tax Rate*, Working paper 7767, National Bureau of Economic Research (Cambridge, Mass., June 2000).

63. The earnings limitations still apply to social security recipients under age 65. Prior to the recent change in the law, the limitation didn't apply once a recipient reached age 70.

64. The Concord Coalition is a nonpartisan organization founded by former Senators Warren Rudman and Paul Tsongas to enhance public discussion of the necessity of reducing federal deficits and other national economic issues and to present and promote fiscal policy alternatives.

65. This shouldn't be confused with maintaining the purchasing power of benefits once a person enrolls in the program—it's not about COLAs. It is about how initial benefits are determined. Initial benefits are calculated by applying a three-bracketed benefit formula to a worker's average earnings—for retirement purposes, a worker's highest 35 years of earnings are counted. The formula's bend points are adjusted annually for wage growth, as are much if not all of a newly eligible retiree's wage record (each year of earnings prior to age 60 is indexed). Because the benefit formula is tilted to give larger returns in its lowest brackets, the indexing of the bend points keeps workers from having more of their earnings computed into benefits at the lower rates applicable to the higher brackets.

66. See statement of Henry Aaron, Gardner Ackley, Mary Falvey, John Porter, and J. W. Van Gorkom, in *Social Security Financing and Benefits, Report of the 1979 Advisory Council* (U.S. Government Printing Office, Washington, D.C., 1979), pp. 212–215.

67. Ibid.

68. This is the approximate present value of the system's projected 75-year deficit. It represents the amount of money needed today that when allowed to grow with interest would be sufficient to fund the projected shortfall.

69. Even where not constructed as a carve out but as a charge against the government's general fund—e.g., as under the Archer-Shaw plan—the *linking* through the clawback represents a *symbolic* first step by reducing social security benefits or funding them based on or with annuities from the individual accounts.

70. Although there are a number of conceptual 401(k)-like models, the federal employees Thrift Savings Plan (TSP) may provide an initial framework around which the new accounts could be designed. The TSP has five different investment funds, including "indexed" stock and bond funds; allows for limited switching; provides for automatic payroll deductions; and has constraints on preretirement withdrawals. Obviously, among numerous other design issues, a system formulated to incorporate "social insurance" concepts might preclude any withdrawals prior to the social security retirement age, death, or disability and mandate periodic payments over lump sums.

Technically speaking, there would be a number of ways as well to constrain the growth of social security benefits, but among the simplest and most uniform would be to make a permanent change to the way *initial* benefits are determined. Under current law, initial benefits for new recipients are computed by multiplying a three-part benefit formula against a worker's average "indexed" monthly earnings (for retirement purposes, the highest 35 years' worth are used). A new formula is created each year for each new group of "eligibles" that reflects increases in the two points separating the three parts of the formula—increases paralleling the rise in average wages nationally. As envisioned here, the social security "wage indexing" series—a benchmark series of annual increases in average national wages (maintained by the Social Security Administration)—would no longer be used to (1) raise the so-called bend points in the formula and (2) adjust (or index) recipients' earnings records for purposes of computing their average earnings. A new indexing series would be constructed to increase the bend points and wage records by an amount sufficient to keep up with inflation the benefits of a newly eligible recipient. As with the current series, the social security actuaries would determine and promulgate this amount annually. To illustrate how it would work, the benefit level for a worker with a record of average wages retiring at age 65 in January 1999 was $953 a month. For a comparable worker retiring in January 2000, it was $987 a month—3.6 percent higher than that of the previous year's retiree. If the January 2000 retiree's benefit had only kept up with inflation, it would have risen to $975 a month, or by 2.3 percent over that of the 1999 retiree. Thus, the current law benefit rules allowed a real increase of 1.3 percent in the purchasing power of the later retiree's benefits ($987 − $975 = $12; $12/$953 = 1.3 percent). Under the procedure envisioned here, the actuaries would have determined by what factor the indexing series needed to be raised to produce a benefit of $975. To phase in the change in the least disruptive manner, the first year of the new series would simply adjust and follow the last year of the old one.

71. The suggestion here is not that it is this author's view that the most feasible reform package is limited to these two measures. The perspective here is that these two measures, or variants thereof, are potentially viable responses to the most critical issues. Other measures, including revenue-generating ones such as raising the maximum amount of earnings subject to social security taxation and provisions to enhance protections for aged survivors and address poverty concerns generally, may also be critical to formulating a politically viable reform package.

# Index

## ABOUT THE AUTHOR

DAVID KOITZ prepared this document while on a leave of absence from the Congressional Research Service of the Library of Congress. Mr. Koitz has had a 30-year career of public service, most of it as a nonpartisan analyst of federal social programs. He has been with the Congressional Research Service since 1979 and over the years has worked extensively with House Ways and Means and Senate Finance Committees on social security matters.